Digital Agency in Higher Educati

C000154578

Exploring how digital resources are being used to engage students in learning and improve educational quality, *Digital Agency in Higher Education* promotes an awareness of relations and interplay between humans and digital artifacts.

Examining the impacts in higher education through experience-based knowledge and a conceptual framework, this book:

- provides a detailed analysis of how transformative agency can be identified, enacted, and cultivated,
- offers up-to-date cases and a future-orientated perspective on technology and knowledge work,
- addresses fundamental assumptions about how teacher education has needed to and needs to continue to develop,
- explores issues of epistemology and ethics when facing increasingly 'intelligent' technologies, and
- argues for transformative agency to place a firm focus on human interests.

Essential reading for teachers in higher education and educational researchers with an interest in how technologies impact learning and teaching, *Digital Agency in Higher Education* uses cutting-edge research to bridge the gap between theoretical perspectives and practices.

Toril Aagaard is associate professor in pedagogy at the Faculty of Humanities, Sports and Educational Science, University of South-Eastern Norway.

Andreas Lund is a professor at the Department of Teacher Education and School Research, University of Oslo, Norway.

Digital Agency in Higher Education

Transforming Teaching and Learning

Toril Aagaard and Andreas Lund

Routledge
Taylor & Francis Group

LONDON AND NEW YORK

First published 2020
by Routledge
2 Park Square, Milton Park, Abingdon, Oxon, OX14 4RN

and by Routledge
605 Third Avenue, New York, NY 10017

First issued in paperback 2022

Routledge is an imprint of the Taylor & Francis Group, an informa business

British Library Cataloguing-in-Publication Data
A catalogue record for this book is available from the British Library

Library of Congress Cataloging-in-Publication Data
A catalogue record has been requested for this book

ISBN: 978-1-03-240094-5 (pbk)
ISBN: 978-0-367-07413-5 (hbk)
ISBN: 978-0-429-02062-9 (ebk)

DOI: 10.4324/9780429020629

Typeset in Times New Roman
by codeMantra

Contents

Acknowledgments   *viii*

Introduction   1

1   Transforming higher education: what is at stake?   3
   Challenges and the need for agency 3
   Transformative agency 7
         Double stimulation – an analytical concept 8
   Digitalization has epistemological consequences 10
   References 14

2   Digital technologies: tools, artifacts, and affordances   18
   Before and after takeoff 18
   Theoretical point of departure 19
   From tools to artifacts 20
   Affordances 23
   References 25

3   Educational quality, transformation, and digitalization   28
   The elephant 28
   Cluster concepts 29
   Quality as transformation 30
   "What remains unsaid" – a project with
      transformative qualities 33
   Connecting the dots: what does the literature say? 35
   Quality work involving a chain of agents 37
   It's elephants all the way down! 39
   References 40

**4 Digitalization, quality, and policy: the case of
a White Paper** 42

Introducing case 42
The missing links 42
Method 45
Findings 46
  Digitalization and educational quality 46
  How are educational quality and
    digitalization connected and described? 47
  Means to enhance digitalization and
    educational quality 48
  Management 49
So what? 49
References 53

**5 Affordances of digital technologies in pedagogical
practices: a review** 55

Investigating affordances 55
Review and findings 56
Educational models 58
21st-century skills – and beyond 62
  Digital learning resources 65
Affordances challenging inertia 67
References 68

6 A response to digitalization: professional digital competence 71

Competence, mastery, and appropriation 71
The many faces of 'digital competence' 73
  TPACK 74
  DigCompEdu 75
  The SAMR model 76
  Professional digital competence 77
References 81

**7 Transforming teacher education – analysis of
transformative initiatives** 84

*Case 1: PDC and transformative agency in a
  small private online community 86*
  About DTESR 86

Developing PDC in teacher education 88
  Vignette 1: integrating different knowledge types 89
  Vignette 2: bridging in-school and
    out-of-school contexts 91
  Vignette 3: committing to research-based
    approaches 93
Synthesizing 94
Case 2: the LUDO project 95
About LUDO 96
  Vignette 1: seed projects 98
  Vignette 2: employing teachers from
    schools in teacher education 99
  Vignette 3: from micro initiatives to
    institutional change 100
Synthesizing 103
References 104

8   Can we educate students for a future we do not know?   107
Epistemologies 111
The agentive student and the teacher as designer 113
Ethical considerations and dilemmas 115
References 117

Index   *119*

Acknowledgments

The authors thank Ann-Therese Arstorp for her valuable feedback on the manuscript for this book and Live Kristiane Sveva for her help with practical issues. They also thank the eDU research group at the University of South-Eastern Norway; the TEPEC research group and the ProTed Center of Excellence at the Department of Teacher Education and School Research, University of Oslo; and our colleagues at both universities. Much of the material in this book is indebted to their ideas and work. The same goes for colleagues at the Norwegian Agency for International Cooperation and Quality Enhancement in Higher Education (DIKU).

Introduction

If you study or work at a higher education (HE) institution, you are already acquainted with digital resources and digitally dependent practices – a phenomenon we in this book refer to as digitalization. You use a smartphone, a laptop, or a smartboard to stay in touch with fellow students or colleagues and check relevant web pages. As a lecturer, you can use such resources to activate students with student response systems to 'flip' your classes, and as a student, you can interact with scientific libraries and archives and cowrite papers in real time.

This book takes you down a slightly different path. It is little used, therefore sometimes hard to find; there are obstacles, unexpected curves; and sometimes the forest is dense. It is a demanding walk. Nevertheless, we hope the reward is a fascinating scenery, unexpected views, and a feeling of empowerment.

We are talking about connecting digitalization to knowledge work and educational quality; we argue for transformative agency in the face of digitalization, suggest principles for the professional digital competence needed to do all this, and acknowledge the many ethical dilemmas along the way. We also try to develop and establish a common language, a discourse that can serve to guide HE policies and practices.

We have already referred to 'digital resources', not tools or instruments due to their instrumental and reductionist overtones. By 'digital resources' we mean digital technologies, digitalized services, and digital content. Boundaries between these are blurred, and the combinations are many: gamification, health chips, collaborative writing, student response systems, robotics, etc. – the list is infinite. Digital resources develop at breathtaking speed, and with such power, that HE needs to analyze and follow up on the epistemological implications of digitalization. What does digitalization mean for high-level knowledge work? Which digital practices should HE be prepared for, which should be encouraged and fostered, and which should be avoided and opposed? Questions like these emerge in digital contexts, and there is a pressing need for HE institutions to respond to them.

By connecting digitalization to knowledge work and epistemic practices, we introduce a number of issues and concepts that in themselves would merit a book. We theorize digital resources as artifacts, highlight affordances that emerge, discuss connections between digitalization and educational quality, consider ethical dilemmas that emerge in a digitalized society, and present literature reviews as well as some selected cases. Ironically, in a series that carries the term 'focus' as a common denominator, we operate with a crowded focus. The reason is that it is the connections between the themes that matter, much more than the mere sum of them. It is in the connections we find properties that the separate themes lack.

Still, our response to the challenges briefly touched upon above is transformative agency. Therefore, this theme is running through the book. Transformative agency means not succumbing to digitalization as something predestined or out of our control; it implies to meet problematic situations and daunting issues that require interplay between humans and digital resources for educational purposes.

We hope that the book will raise the readers' awareness of what is at stake in HE due to digitalization. Our aim is to contribute to mustering the agency that scholars, decision makers, and students need in order to firmly place human interests and the knowledge producing sectors in focus when facing the digital surge.

1 Transforming higher education

What is at stake?

Challenges and the need for agency

It is easy to ridicule universities and colleges as historical leftovers, Jurassic Parks where academic dinosaurs lecture students in plenaries that have not changed for a century or more (see, e.g., Kak, 2018, for argument and ensuing online debate). To some extent, it is true: Few institutions have been more stable, conservative, and even inert than the ones responsible for higher education (HE), especially when faced with digitalization (e.g., Bates & Sangrà, 2011; Selwyn, 2010). They have been committed and unwavering public, democratic institutions cultivating the argument, reasoning, and scientific knowledge that have become cornerstones of academic life and foundations for decision-making (Ellis & McNicholl, 2015; Jónasson, 2016; Selwyn, 2014). However, over the past few decades, many institutions have increasingly engaged in financial competition, neoliberalism, and aggressive capitalism, threatening the historically heralded commitments of HE (Ellis & McNicholl, 2015; Schulze-Cleven, Reitz, Maesse & Angermuller, 2017; Shumar, 1997). It is at the juxtaposition of tradition and recent market orientation we find HE coming to terms with digitalization – a development with tremendous force and with epistemic, social, and ethical implications that require principled strategies and transformative action.

One of the deep and wide-ranging changes is how HE has developed from being elite institutions to becoming institutions of mass education. New teaching and learning opportunities arise as digital technologies are transformational as well as disruptive (Lucas, 2016). Making education accessible and flexible to a broad range of people is among many opportunities that arise in digital societies. A romanticized optimism sometimes characterizes beliefs about the potentials of digitalization in HE, for example, when it comes to how Massive Open Online Courses (MOOCs) and other distributed models in HE promote accessibility and motivate people to take education (Carey, 2016). As we show in Chapter 5, other researchers are critical and claim that such models lead to 'commodification' and reduce educational quality. For instance, the high complexity of MOOCs is a challenge (Buhl, 2018; Gil-Jaurena & Dominquez, 2018), and scaling up with thousands of students participating, it gets hard to engage so many in systematic intellectual development and critical thinking. Ellis and McNicholl (2015) invoked notions of 'academic capitalism' with its proletarianization of faculty and emphasis on exchange values.

Without taking on a comprehensive review of literature on the digitalization of HE, a look at four relevant works can provide insights, from different angles, into how digitalization materializes in HE. The first study (Lillejord, Børte, Nesje, & Rud, 2018) focuses on digitalization and active learning, the second (Bates & Sangrà, 2011) addresses the process of integrating digital technology into HE, the third (Selwyn, 2014) discusses digitalization from an ideological power perspective, and the last (Jónasson, 2016) identifies forces that seem to influence transformation of knowledge work in HE. We do not assert that these studies are 'representative' of the total situation, but they make visible some of the educational, organizational, ideological, and epistemological questions that emerge in HE due to digital development.

First, we look at a recent systematic review made by a group of researchers (Lillejord et al., 2018) in which the following question was asked: "How can teaching with technology support student active learning in higher education?" (p. 2). Thus, a specific link between digitalization and a specific pedagogical approach is forged with a focus on *how* digital resources are used. The rationale for their review is found in the EU Commission's report that highlights the need for new modes of learning and teaching across HE institutions (European Commission, 2014). An elaborate search algorithm yielded 6,526 academic articles from search databases. Based on exclusion and inclusion criteria, the amount was strongly reduced leaving the group with 35 high-quality studies from 2012 to 2018. These were subject to a configurative synthesis, which again gave reasons to conclude that transmission-oriented teaching in lecture halls still dominates, despite recent trends in 'flipped' practices. Thus, even if digitalization carries high expectations, in particular when it comes to promoting student activity, HE seems to have heterogeneous follow-up strategies. The study showed that there are still too few empirical studies on digitalization in HE and that there is a need for more longitudinal, iterative studies. The researchers also identified a paradox that "academics appear not be using a *scholarly approach* when implementing technology in education" (p. 4, emphasis in original).

Second, a study of over 30 universities and colleges in the United States and Europe investigated how they integrated digital technologies into their practices (Bates & Sangrà, 2011). It showed that HE institutions were cautious and that there was a distinct gap between leadership and faculty engaging in technology-rich practices. Where digital technologies were part of strategic plans, they were integrated into existing practices and strategies and rarely as change agents. The authors focused on integration of administrative and teaching services, management of digital resources, training of technology managers and administrators, and quality assurance methods, with a view to academic practices. They also emphasized increasing flexible access to students and faculty and cost-effectiveness. Their book shows how digitalization potentially can transform HE (from leadership and quality assurance to e-learning), but that the institutions so far have mostly focused on organizational and administrative dimensions.

Third, in Selwyn's (2014) thought-provoking book, *Digital Technology and the Contemporary University*, digitalization is discussed in light of ideology and power structures, more as a sociopolitical impulse than as a pedagogical change agent. He addresses the clash between "bricks and mortar campuses" and a complex and rapidly developing technology and how this brings about tensions and even breakdowns, especially between the leadership who often cultivate tradition (or fight for market shares) and the future-oriented teaching staff who develop practices. On a systemic level, he finds that Information and Communication Technology (ICT) often is used to replicate practices in HE instead of transforming them, it opens up for an inflated audit culture, and is increasingly taxing on academics. For example, it makes academics available 24/7 (emails, virtual meetings, just-in-time supervision, etc.) and working hours become ubiquitous through increased (perceived or articulated) demand for immediate digital response to work-related matters. Consequently, Selwyn sees a "need to engage with the politics of higher education and technology" (p. 121), and argues that "it is necessary to counter the digital hype that pervades higher education with more socially focused and publically minded concerns" (p. 141). Selwyn convincingly maps the territory and points to paths forward where HE institutions (HEIs) do not only give in to winds of change but continue to cultivate democratic values and high-quality epistemic work.

Finally, Jónasson (2016) approaches change in HE from a more knowledge-oriented or epistemic position, claiming that traditional disciplines are challenged by "new knowledge which may often be outside the traditional disciplines" and that "a host of new skills may be relevant for the world of tomorrow" (p. 1). When Jónasson moves on to identify the forces that impede what we might call epistemic transformation, he finds "general conservativism, system stability, standards, fuzziness of new ideas, the strength of old ideas, vested interests, lack of space and motivation for initiative, and lack of consequence of no change" (p. 1). This amounts to a view where institutional infrastructure and staff involvement are seen as the main inertial constraints for knowledge and content development. Jónasson raises a discussion as to *how* HE can change and points to epistemic work and the agentive role of 'professionals', i.e., educators, in such work.

None of the studies referred to above argues that digitalization is the panacea for institutional or educational transformation although they acknowledge a transformative potential. Only Jónasson's analysis addresses epistemic issues, but without taking on vital issues of epistemology in itself. One reason may be that he does not address digitalization as a specifically transformative force and/or the type of agency required to make it serve educational goals. On the other hand, he identifies teacher education as the sole academic program representing inertia, thus unsuspectingly setting the stage for the theme of the present volume: the epistemological implications of digitalization in HE.

Despite the various approaches in the literature above, they all add to the picture of HE institutions as difficult to change. Together, they identify some reasons why digitalization in HE is challenging, for instance too much focus on infrastructure, insufficient leadership and hesitancy among professional staff to develop new epistemic practices.

Our point of departure is that digitalization makes it possible to expand educational repertoires and break out of status quo. This is not technological determinism. Transformation of HE does not happen without human agency and with ethical and epistemological considerations to accompany it. Therefore, we argue, transformative agency and epistemological implications of people's access to and use of digital technologies emerge as pressing concerns for HE.

The relationship between human agents and digital technologies is historically new, not stable, and often under-theorized. In Chapter 2, we present perspectives that clarify connections and relations. In the remainder of this chapter, we turn to a conceptual framework and theoretical perspective that we argue has explanatory power when being confronted with the complex phenomenon of digitalization and transformation in HE. We elaborate what we mean by transformative agency and discuss digitalization with a view to epistemological consequences.

Transformative agency

As noted above, we argue that human agency is decisive in what form digitalization takes and what educational objectives it serves. This is contrary to technological determinism whether romantic or dystopic. Agency is a prerequisite for conscious transformation. In an age where algorithms have become extremely powerful and sophisticated, we have found the need to emphasize human, transformative agency in HE (see, e.g., Harari, 2017, for dazzling and provocative perspectives on nonhuman agency and absence of free will).

Agency can be productively applied in research on agents encountering change. The notion of change has developed in the *Journal of Educational Change* (JEC). From a top-down and large-scale approach, recent years have seen more empirically driven, participatory-oriented, and methodologically advanced approaches (Garcia-Huidobro, Nannemann, Bacon, & Thompson, 2017). According to Garcia-Huidobro et al. (2017), "at a time of rapid educational innovation, it is no exaggeration to say that a lack of theorization around meaningful conceptualizations of educational change constitutes a crisis in the field" (p. 289). The present volume can be read as a response to such a crisis.

Often, Emirbayer and Mische's article titled "What Is Agency?" (1998) is referred to when unpacking the notion of agency. At the heart of their conceptualization is "the capacity of human beings to shape circumstances in which they live" (p. 965). There is a dialectic and dynamic relationship between agent and context. Thus, agency is transformative and affects the situation but also the agent. Further, Emirbayer and Mische see agency as having a projective (future) dimension and quote Dewey (1981) where he links agency to a capacity to "read future results in present on-goings" (p. 69). However, the authors do not examine the cultural resources that may be activated in order to mediate such agency, a vital principle in our approach as well as in cultural–historical approaches in general.

The transformative dimensions introduced by Emirbayer and Mische (1998) have been refined by several scholars. Mäkitalo (2016), in a special issue on agency, defines the concept as "the capacity of humans to distance themselves from their *immediate* surroundings and it implies recognition of the possibility to intervene in, and transform the meaning of, situated activities" (p. 64, emphasis in original). In line with this approach, we also adhere to the construct of transformative agency, defined by Virkkunen (2006) as "breaking away from the given frame of action and taking the initiative to transform it" (p. 233). This sets transformative agency apart from mere decision-making. Sannino (2015a), also drawing on Virkkunen, outlined the following challenge: "How this type of agency comes into being, how it evolves and how it can be nurtured should be the object of careful analysis and constructive scholarly debates" (p. 1).

Double stimulation – an analytical concept

To examine transformative agency and link it to the kind of competence that we argue is needed in HE, we draw on Vygotsky's (1978) principle of double stimulation (see also Sannino, 2015a, 2015b; Sannino & Engeström, 2017) and on cultural–historical perspectives (e.g., Arievitch, 2017; Engeström, 1987; Engeström, Miettinen, & Punamäki, 1999; Kaptelinin & Nardi, 2006; Roth, 2004; Stetsenko & Arievitch, 2010). In Chapter 7, this principle is analytically operationalized in two case studies of transformative initiatives in teacher education. In the following, the principle's theoretical underpinnings are discussed.

The double stimulation principle involves a first stimulus (S1) that represents a problem, conflict of motives, challenge, dilemma, uncertainty, an impasse, etc., which requires agency to break out of or resolve such situations. Agents make use of or even develop second stimuli (S2), i.e., resources that are available or constructed, mobilized, and put to use in an effort to solve the S1. The classic example is the use of a watch to decide when to break out of and, thus, transform a situation that is perceived as meaningless because waiting seems to go on indeterminately ("I will stand up and leave if something has not happened by 2.30") (Sannino & Laitinen, 2015). A more relevant example for our focus is the recurrent dissatisfaction with the traditional lecture format. Numerous studies (e.g., O'Neill & McMahon, 2005) show that students are not engaged beyond passive listening, their attendance rates are poor, and lecturers have found it difficult to break out of such situations due to historically entrenched, often monologic, practices framed by 45-minute time slots and the architecture of auditoriums. In Vygotsky's terms, this is a classic S1 since the lecturers wish to change or there is a demand for change, but the path or the way to create this change seems uncertain.

However, the S1 can be resolved if the lecturers make use of or develop a (series of) S2. A resource can be, e.g., various ways of 'flipping' the lecture so that students and educators can devote more time to interaction, while information and content presentation are left to video clips. Also digital student response systems are potential resources that can be used as simple 'clickers' or to facilitate more sophisticated enactment in the form of real-time questions and 'hot topics' in discussions. Such second stimuli may be material, conceptual or symbolic artifacts, or social in the shape of diverse types of interaction and collaboration. The crucial element is not so much the resource in itself but how it is put to use through volitional action. Also, note that it is important to see the S2 not as a singular stimulus or 'quick fix' but a series of stimuli, leaving a trail of agentic endeavors. Thus, complex and technology-rich environments afford multiple tools – the question is which tools are picked up and appropriated by learners. We argue that the double stimulation principle has explanatory power when analyzing and acting in problem situations where a series of complex resources (S2) is put to use.

We deviate somewhat from Vygotsky's original experimental approaches to double stimulation. Where Vygotsky regarded S2 as *neutral*, we argue that second stimuli are inscribed with intentions for use. For instance, wikis hold collaborative intentions, student response systems are developed to create and sustain engagement, virtual worlds intentionally suspend limitations in the real worlds, learning analytics afford more valid assessment by visualizing (and – controversially – prescribing) learning trajectories, etc. However, agents (e.g., programmers, developers) also instill them with their own intentions.

Finally, an important point is made regarding double stimulation; the relationship between the problem situation (S1) and the potentially useful resources (S2) is dialectic. The principle is linked to situations where we experience tensions and contradictions. This implies that a series of S2, when successfully put to use, serves to transform the original problem situation, S1, e.g., when activating with a passive group of students. Note that not merely the situation has changed, but also the agent(s) experiencing it. Having 'lived' the experiencing of transformative agency the agent is not identical to who he/she was before. This resonates with Heraclitus's (544 BC) famous maxim that "You cannot step into the same river twice because you are changing and the river is changing". Interestingly, other versions have the last part as "...for other waters are continually flowing on." Metaphorically, this could easily capture the perpetual influx of digital resources as they, too, represent a continuously changing river pooling into the educational ocean and changing the conditions under which students are learning and do epistemic work.

So far, in this chapter, our intention has been to argue that the educational possibilities and challenges that emerge with the digitalization of HE call for transformative agency. Such agency involves reciprocity and interaction between the individual, the collective, and the contexts, and use of cultural resources (material, discursive and symbolic) as mediating artifacts for transformative purposes. The principle of double stimulation is introduced because of its explanatory power when analyzing what agents (students, educators) invest in and struggle with in order to make sense of uncertainty and challenging situations where they need to make difficult choices and break away from or transform practices.

In this volume, the challenging situation (S1) amounts to how HE deals with both the potential educational risks and benefits of digitalization. Consequently, transformative agency remains a recurring concept. However, agency does not automatically lead to transformation. For example, abstaining from action to preserve the status quo is also agency but hardly transformative. Transformative agency arises as a necessity when people are placed in demanding situations involving a conflict of motives (S1), thus creating a wish or need to break out of the current situation. Agents perceive these experiences as internal tensions that require critical decisions to transform the status quo (including HE inertia). Participants aim to break away from constraining practices and expand them despite obvious uncertainties about the consequences of this effort. Some of the educational uncertainties and challenges that HE needs to deal with emerge because digital environments affect knowledge work in fundamental ways. This brings us to the next section where we seek to substantiate the claim that digitalization has deep epistemological consequences.

Digitalization has epistemological consequences

When venturing into the realm of epistemology or knowledge theory, it is easy to be caught up in big philosophical questions and debates (e.g., Descartes's rationalism vs. Locke's empiricism), risking conceptual exegesis. We will *not* attempt to do this in the following section. Rather, our aim is to build an argument for why digitalization and digitized educational practices have epistemological consequences.

Epistemology refers to one of several ways we, according to Aristotle, come to know the world: through scientific knowledge (*episteme*). Of course, this particular way of knowing is supplemented with various other types, e.g., practical insight (*phronesis*) and instrumental know-how (*techne*). (For a detailed study of these and more, see, e.g., Broadie & Rowe, 2002). Traditionally, epistemology has responded to questions such as (1) "What is the nature of knowledge?" and "(Where) Is knowledge located?", (2) "How do we come to knowledge?" and "By what means have we come to knowledge?", and (3) "What are the limits of our knowledge?" and "What is the scope and dimension of our knowledge?" (see also Magrini, 2009). While the questions have remained constant, scholars observe that over the past decade, epistemology has come to gravitate towards the value of *understanding* rather than *knowledge* (Carter & Kotzee, 2015; Pritchard, 2013). In this volume, it is the second type of questions that preoccupy us, although we also discuss the first type.

Our conception of knowing, understanding and learning influences our educational practices. We work with our students through assignments, activities, and assessment according to our epistemological dispositions, e.g., that knowledge is experienced, transferred, discovered, constructed, or, a result of dialogue, mediated activity or pure logic. In educational practices, we (educators as well as students) design for, operationalize, instigate, sustain, and assess activities that advance agents' present status of insights, i.e., we engage in epistemic work. In HE, such epistemic work has to deal with research-based knowledge, i.e., knowledge that is subject to a rapid turnover rate due to the global increase in research and digital access to it. And although the task of measuring the increase in research seems daunting, estimates suggest that global scientific output doubles every nine years (Van Noorden, 2014), not to be confused with the doubling rate of (dis) information which is down to hours. One of the driving forces behind increased growth and turnover rate of what is considered valid and research-based knowledge is digitalization and digital archives. Already in 2003, Lankshear observed that digitalization involved changes in the phenomena we study, changes in our conceptions of knowledge and knowing, changes in ourselves as 'knowers', and changes in the relative significance of types of knowing (pp. 167–168). Since then, digitalization has brought about new challenges and concerns related to what we (need to) learn.

Digitalization plays a vital role when we design new educational spaces, workplaces, cars, kitchens, and not least spaces and sources of entertainment. Objects with intent (OwIs) such as a ball programmed to respond to a child's agency, a jacket that makes you feel safe by responding to body signals of nervousness, or a bedside lamp that lulls you into sleep become embedded in human activity as collaborative partners (Rozendaal, Boon, & Kaptelinin, 2019). In other words, digitalization is increasingly *embedded* in both mundane and scientific practices to the extent that they are ubiquitous but invisible. However, the consequence is that humans as social agents also become increasingly embedded in practices, situations, and spaces permeated by digitalization. Hybridity – the blurring of boundaries between physical and virtual contexts – is on the rise. For example, a researcher or student finding a particular paper on, e.g., "educational quality" in a digital research database is immediately presented with a vast number of potentially just as relevant papers to be accessed and downloaded. Embeddedness also explains the everyday experience of being contacted by a party offering to sell you something that the party already knows you are interested in (from having tracked your keystrokes over time). This is made possible by just one simple algorithm that testifies to such embeddedness; your personality is to some extent shaped by your 'likes'. This is, of course, big business and potentially paves the way for manipulation of our beliefs, attitudes, and values. In this way, digital technologies structure our cognition (Huebner, 2013). In line with Jónasson (2016), we argue that embeddedness challenges traditional epistemic positions in HE – the idea that knowledge is a "package" of content that in a comprised version can be presented in the shape of a reading list. Moreover, embeddedness incites HE to discuss new ways of assessing students' competencies as 'performative' (Säljö, 2010), i.e., how students exploit pervasive digital resources. Thus, the first principle that links digitalization with epistemology is *embeddedness*.

Digitalization is not only embedded, but it is also becoming *embodied*. We take for granted that our mind influences our bodily actions, but may not always give proper consideration to how our bodies influence the way our minds work. In other words, our senses and bodies enable us to interact with and make sense of the world, be cognizant, and thus develop (in a broad sense). For instance, analyzing music, art, crafts, and aesthetics can find explanatory power in embodied approaches. Note that this is an extremely reductionist presentation of a broad and diverse field (Shapiro, 2007). Our point is that embodied cognition increasingly involves digitalization. That artifacts have extended our cognitive capacities is nothing new: glasses, hearing aids, and pacemakers have been here for ages, the first-generation "wearables". But when we now have access to glasses with augmented reality (AR) functions and implants (microchips, 'healthcare chips') that analyze blood sugar and cholesterol levels and even capture cancer cells and send the data to our cell phones, technologies are not merely add-ons but integrated agents that monitor our existence and influence our decisions. And although the 'Deadline' app and health chip technology predicting life expectancy based on your current lifestyle and medical condition may be in their infancy and appear somewhat crude ("Happy holidays! You're going to die by 67"), it offers an intriguing/frightening glimpse of what is ahead. In this way, digitized information becomes internalized in our biological and cognitive endeavors (Lynch, 2014). These perspectives raise extremely important ethical issues: When is shared information beneficial? Will insurance companies have access to such information? We are not merely being monitored by satellites and CCTV but carry potential spyware in our bodies. Consequently, embodiment of digital technology is the second principle that connects digitalization to epistemology. This phenomenon challenges HE programs as to decide how to prepare students for both working life and a social presence with ethical dilemmas that arise as digital technology becomes increasingly embodied.

Unlike embodied cognition, *extended* cognition is perhaps the more conventional way of thinking about digitalization – how pocket calculators, spellcheckers, smartphones, and a plethora of extremely sophisticated instruments have increasingly taken on more cognitive load and served to engage with humans in distributed cognition (Hutchins, 1995, is a prime example). Extended cognition, too, come with some fascinating or disturbing perspectives. For example, through so-called machine learning, a digitalized system can be fed with all existing X-ray photos of cancer and/or medical journals and studies that it might detect cancer in new X-ray photos that the human doctor might not. Such distributed or extended intelligence will have consequences for treatment, hopes, and predictions. Another example is the car that takes control over a situation where a head-on collision potentially involving several passengers is avoided by swerving across the sidewalk, killing an elderly pedestrian. Who programmed the car – a professorial team of moral philosophers, computer scientists, or people from insurance companies? Regardless of programmer(s), the car is given extended cognition and can decide on the outcome of the accident. The knowledge that, in turn, is activated with potentially fatal consequences is located outside human minds. This phenomenon, too, generates ethical dilemmas. In HE a common concern is that extended cognition makes students less motivated to remember things and read academic texts. Others suggest that extended cognition calls for educational programs that foster 'performative competence' (Säljö, 2010), i.e., where students learn through appropriating and using artifacts while solving real-life problems.

The categories embedded, embodied, and extended are not discrete or without grey areas, but they might still help us analyze and reflect on the complex relations between humans and digital technologies, including epistemological and ethical implications. For example, 'smart diapers' that analyze babies' poop to inform parents in daily care can be said to reflect all categories. Regardless of categorization and although the example might seem innocent enough, it might also place the unsuspecting infant in the hands outside of parental control including giant genetic databases.

This admittedly superficial engagement with epistemological perspectives shows that we come to knowledge by engaging with digital technologies that are embedded and embodied, and that extend our cognition. Epistemology depends on the social interaction between agents and the social practices we engage in to advance and share knowledge (Kotzee, 2013). The implication is that we encounter multiple and very different epistemologies that are context dependent (Bricker & Bell, 2016). For example, students' serious gaming follows a very different epistemic route (competition, scores, winning, etc.) than researchers' controlled experiments (replicability, generalizability, trustworthiness, etc.). Digitalization changes our capacities to do epistemic work. The possibilities are daunting, but so are the risks. That is why HEIs have extraordinary responsibility for approaching digitalization in ways that involve more than administrative tools, infrastructure, and course design. As Pritchard (2013) emphasizes, *understanding* may serve as a more appropriate epistemic goal for education than knowledge. Understanding is process oriented, always evolving, and always malleable. However, fostering understanding in networked and digitalized HEIs (and beyond) requires a more principled view of the digital technologies involved, and this will be the theme of Chapter 2.

References

Arievitch, I. M. (2017). *Beyond the Brain. An Agentive Activity Perspective on Mind, Development and Learning.* Rotterdam, NE: Sense Publishers.

Bates, A. W., & Sangrà, A. (2011). *Managing Technology in Higher Education: Strategies for Transforming Teaching and Learning.* San Francisco, CA: Jossey-Bass.

Bricker, L. A., & Bell, P. (2016). Exploring Images of Epistemic Cognition across Contexts and Over Time. In J. A. Greene, W. A. Sandoval & I. Bråten (Eds.), *Handbook of Epistemic Cognition* (pp. 197–214). New York, NY: Routledge.

Broadie, S., & Rowe, C. (Eds.). (2002). *Aristotle: Nicomachean Ethics: Translation, Introduction, Commentary.* Oxford: Oxford University Press.

Buhl, M. (2018). Upscaling the Number of Learners, Fragmenting the Role of Teachers: How Do Massive Open Online Courses (MOOCs) Form New Conditions for Learning Design? *International Review of Education, 64*(2), 179–195. doi:10.1007/s11159-018-9714-1

Carey, K. (2016). *The End of College: Creating the Future of Learning and the University of Everywhere.* New York, NY: Riverhead Books.

Carter, J. A., & Kotzee, B. (2015). Epistemology of Education. Retrieved October 15, 2018, from Oxford Bibliographies Online https://philpapers. org/archive/CAREOE-4.pdf

Dewey, J. (1981). The Need for a Recovery of Philosophy. In John J. McDermott (Ed.), *The Philosophy of John Dewey* (pp. 58–97). Chicago: University of Chicago Press.

Ellis, V., & McNicholl, J. (2015). *Transforming Teacher Education: Reconfiguring the Academic Work*. London; New Delhi; New York, NY; Sydney: Bloomsbury Academic.

Emirbayer, M., & Mische, A. (1998). What Is Agency? *American Journal of Sociology, 103*(4), 962–1023.

Engeström, Y. (1987). *Learning by Expanding: An Activity-Theoretical Approach to Developmental Research*. Helsinki: Orienta-Konsultit Oy.

Engeström, Y., Miettinen, R., & Punamäki, R. (Eds.). (1999). *Perspectives on Activity Theory*. Cambridge: Cambridge University Press.

European Commission. (2014). *Report to the European Commission on New Modes of Learning and Teaching in Higher Education*. Luxembourg: European Commission.

Garcia-Huidobro, J. C., Nannemann, A., Bacon, C. K., & Thompson, K. (2017). Evolution in Educational Change: A Literature Review of the Historical Core of the *Journal of Educational Change*. *Journal of Educational Change, 18*, 263–293. doi:10.1007/s10833-017-9298-8

Gil-Jaurena, I., & Domínguez, D. (2018). Teachers' Roles in Light of Massive Open Online Courses (MOOCs): Evolution and Challenges in Higher Distance Education. *International Review of Education, 64*(2), 197–219. doi:10.1007/s11159-018-9715-0

Harari, Y. N. (2017). *Homo Deus*. London: Vintage.

Huebner, B. (2013). Socially Embedded Cognition. *Cognitive Systems Research, 25–26*, 13–18.

Hutchins, E. (1995). *Cognition in the Wild*. Cambridge, MA: MIT Press.

Jónasson, J. T. (2016). Educational Change, Inertia and Potential Futures. Why Is It Difficult to Change the Content of Education? *European Journal of Futures Research, 4*(7), 1–14. doi:10.1007/s40309-016-0087-z

Kak, S. (2018, January 10). Will Traditional Colleges and Universities Become Obsolete? Smithsonian.com. Retrieved July 7, 2019, from https://www. smithsonianmag.com/innovation/will-traditional-colleges-universities-become-obsolete-180967788/

Kaptelinin, V., & Nardi, B. A. (2006). *Acting with Technology: Activity Theory and Interaction Design*. Cambridge, MA; London: MIT Press.

Kotzee, B. (2013). Introduction: Education, Social Epistemology and Virtue Epistemology. *Journal of Philosophy of Education, 47*(2), 157–167.

Lankshear, C. (2003). The Challenge of Digital Epistemologies. *Education, Communication & Information, 3*(2), 167–186. doi:10.1080/14636310303144

Lillejord, S., Børte, K., Nesje, K., & Rud, E. (2018). *Learning and Teaching with Technology in Higher Education – A Systematic Review*. Oslo, NO: Knowledge Centre for Education.

Lucas, H. C. (2016). *Technology and the Disruption of Higher Education.* London: World Scientific Publishing Co.

Lynch, M. P. (2014). Neuromedia, Extended Knowledge and Understanding. *Philosophical Issues, 24,* 299–313. doi:10/1111/phis.12035

Magrini, J. (2009). How the Conception of Knowledge Influences Our Educational Practices: Toward a Philosophical Understanding of Epistemology in Education. Retrieved from http://dc.cod.edu/philosophypub/13

Mäkitalo, Å. (2016). On the Notion of Agency in Studies of Interaction and Learning. *Learning, Culture, and Social Interaction, 10,* 64–67. doi:10.1016/j.lcsi.2016.07003

O'Neill, G., & McMahon, T. (2005). Student-centred Learning: What Does It Mean for Students and Lecturers. In G. O'Neill, S. Moore & B. McMullin (Eds.), *Student-Centred Learning: What Does It Mean for Students and Lecturers* (pp. 27–36). Dublin: AISHE.

Pritchard, D. (2013). Epistemic Virtue and the Epistemology of Education. *Philosophical Issues, 24*(1), 236–247.

Roth, W.-M. (2004). Activity Theory and Education: An Introduction. *Mind, Culture and Activity, 11*(1), 1–8.

Rozendaal, M. C., Boon, B., & Kaptelinin, V. (2019). Objects with Intent: Designing Everyday Things as Collaborative Partners. *ACM Transactions on Computer-Human Interaction, 26*(4), 1–30. doi:10.1145/3325277

Säljö, R. (2010). Digital Tools and Challenges to Institutional Traditions of Learning: Technologies, Social Memory and the Performative Nature of Learning. *Journal of Computer Assisted Learning, 26*(1), 53–64.

Sannino, A. (2015a). The Emergence of Transformative Agency and Double Stimulation: Activity-Based Studies in the Vygotskian Tradition. *Learning, Culture, and Social Interaction, 4,* 1–3. doi:10.1016/j.lcsi.2014.07.001

Sannino, A. (2015b). The Principle of Double Stimulation: A Path to Volitional Action. *Learning, Culture, and Social Interaction, 6,* 1–15. doi:10.1016/j.lcsi.2015.01.001

Sannino, A., & Engeström, Y. (2017). Relational Agency, Double Stimulation, and the Object of Activity: An Intervention Study in a Primary School. In A. Edwards (Ed.), *Working Relationally in and across Practices. A Cultural-Historical Approach to Collaboration* (pp. 43–57). New York, NY: Cambridge University Press.

Sannino, A., & Laitinen, A. (2014). Double Stimulation in the Waiting Experiment: Testing a Vygotskian Model of the Emergence of Volitional Action. *Learning, Culture, and Social Interaction.* doi:10.1016/j.lcsi.2014.07.002

Schulze-Cleven, T., Reitz, T., Maesse, J., & Angermuller, J. (2017). The New Political Economy of Higher Education: Between Distributional Conflicts and Discursive Stratification. *Higher Education, 73,* 795–812.

Selwyn, N. (2010). Looking Beyond Learning: Notes Towards the Critical Study of Educational Technology. *Journal of Computer Assisted Learning, 26,* 65–73.

Selwyn, N. (2014). *Digital Technology and the Contemporary University.* Abingdon; New York, NY: Routledge.

Shapiro, L. (2007). The Embodied Cognition Research Programme. *Philosophy Compass, 2*(2), 338–346. doi:10.1111/j.1747-9991.2007.00064.x

Shumar, W. (1997). *College for Sale. A Critique of the Commodification of Higher Education*. London: Routledge.

Stetsenko, A., & Arievitch, I. M. (2010). Cultural-Historical Activity Theory. Foundational Worldview, Major Principles, and the Relevance of Sociocultural Context. In S. R. Kirschner & J. Martin (Eds.), *The Sociocultural Turn in Psychology. The Contextual Emergence of Mind and Self* (pp. 231–252). New York, NY: Columbia University Press.

Van Noorden, R. (2014, May 7). Global Scientific Output Doubles Every Nine Years. Retrieved from http://blogs.nature.com/news/2014/05/global-scientific-output-doubles-every-nine-years.html

Virkkunen, J. (2006). Dilemmas in Building Shared Transformative Agency. *@ctivités, 3*(1), 43–66.

Vygotsky, L. S. (1978). *Mind in Society: The Development of Higher Psychological Processes*. Cambridge, MA: Harvard University Press.

2 Digital technologies
Tools, artifacts, and affordances

In Chapter 1, our ambition was to show some of the challenges higher education (HE) faces and argue why digitalization requires change as well as transformative agency. The principle of double stimulation was introduced because it can help us understand and study transformative processes. Finally, we argued for the claim that digitalization has epistemological consequences. In this chapter, we present a perspective on digital technologies as artifacts and explain the risks with treating such technologies merely as tools. Further, we introduce affordance as a concept because this (as transformative agency and double stimulation) has explanatory power when analyzing digital practices in HE.

Before and after takeoff

If an airplane encounters an unexpected problem while in the air, one would probably feel more assured if the captain and crew immediately engage in behaviorist safety procedures than call for a plenary meeting in order to reflect on the situation. However, the airplane crew potentially reflecting on and discussing procedures and technicalities before takeoff is seen as a prerequisite for a safe flight. This illustrates a fundamental principle of learning and teaching; that cognition and context, mind, and available resources are inseparable and situated; different situations and learning objectives call for diverse approaches and resources. However, the resources including digital artifacts have often been regarded as 'mere tools', as amplification or simplification of existing practices (Orlikowski & Iacono, 2001).

Thus, digitalization has tended to be under-theorized in education, although the field of computer-supported collaborative learning (CSCL) has contributed significantly (Koschmann, 1996; Stahl, 2006; Strijbos, Kirschner, & Martens, 2004). Therefore, we, in what follows, seek to establish a view where the relationship between digital technologies and epistemic practices materializes. We build such a view on fundamental cultural–historical tenets; our thinking is deeply interwoven with contexts and resources we put to use, whether, e.g., an abacus or a spreadsheet. In human activity, agents, contexts, and artifacts are mutually constitutive of learning and development (Kaptelinin & Nardi, 2006; Säljö, 1999). An individual on a naked island cut off from other people and cultural resources would not be able to accomplish much.

Although digitalization of educational practices may not be quite as dramatic as the in-flight example, we know from research that HE needs to transform but struggles to engage academic staff in principled approaches to how digitalization affects pedagogy (Bates & Sangrà, 2011; de Laat, Lally, Simons, & Wenger, 2006; Lillejord, Børte, Nesje, & Rud, 2018; Stensaker, Maassen, Borgan, Oftebro, & Karseth, 2007). Conceptual clarity and a theoretical understanding of what digital technologies are and how they affect HE might prepare the ground for broader, more principled and sustained engagement. In order to prepare this ground, we have to examine the underlying epistemologies that are inscribed in digital technologies, i.e., their potential power to impact on how people come to knowledge, how knowledge practices are influenced and shaped, and how competencies are documented and assessed.

Theoretical point of departure

In this volume, we mainly draw on perspectives originating from the Vygotskian tradition, i.e., sociocultural and cultural–historical approaches where learning and teaching are seen as activities mediated by cultural tools or artifacts. In addition, cultural context and heritage along with the social dimensions of activity are deeply intertwined with cognitive development (Engeström, Miettinen, & Punamäki, 1999; Vygotsky, 1978; Wertsch, 1998). We also acknowledge contributions from distributed cognition (Hutchins, 1995) and actor–network theory (Latour, 1999) that emphasize the agency of both humans and nonhumans. Also, more recently, Harari (1917) and Tegmark (2017) argue that certain digital technologies and in particular artificial intelligence demonstrate the potential to transform what it means to be human (see also Chapter 8). However, in the present volume, we keep humans and nonhumans ontologically separate. That digital technology has potential power to transform epistemic practices does not imply that digital technologies come with pre-deterministic qualities that cannot be altered by human effort; it is always the actor–artifact relations that shape how social practices emerge and are transformed (Conole, 2008; Shaffer & Clinton, 2006; Wertsch, 1998). Nevertheless, when everything that is digitalized can be accessed, copied, shared, manipulated, and falsified, as well as exercise agency (diagnoses, self-driving cars, etc.), we simply have to acknowledge the epistemic shift we face. We do not pursue this techno-philosophical debate, but see, e.g., Shaffer and Clinton (2006) or Latour (1999) for intriguing perspectives.

From tools to artifacts

Often digital resources are referred to in everyday terms as 'tools'. While it serves to make digitalization familiar and nonintimidating, it comes with certain limitations. A 'tool' is used to make existing practices less tiresome, less time consuming, and more economical without transforming the essentials of the activity. Thus, tools often lend themselves to cost–benefit analyses and measuring effectiveness (learning outcomes, better grades, reduced educational costs per capita, etc.). The tool as an everyday term does not include people's broader intentions of developing or transforming situations and practices. However, the scientific concept '*artifact*' does. As the first syllable in the artifact concept suggests, it is something human-made for certain purposes within a specific cultural–historical context. If we pick up a stone in order to hammer a nail, we operate the stone as a tool. If the stone is polished and shaped in order to please our aesthetic senses or serve as an arrowhead, it has become an artifact with exchange value. The plowshare was developed in order to cultivate land in ways that were not possible until its emergence; it transformed the practice of farming through its expanded use value. At the heart of artifacts is their cultural significance. They are developed over time (such as the plowshare) and are, consequently, carriers of historically and collectively developed insights (Säljö, 1999, 2010). Such insights may be domain specific or they are valid across several domains. Take the mundane speed bump as an example. It carries inscriptions of law (you have to reduce speed), mechanics (if speed is not reduced, your car's suspension may suffer), medicine (at lower speeds there is less risk of severe bodily harm to pedestrians or other motorists), economics (all the previous considerations amount to lower societal costs), and so on.

In Chapter 1, the watch was presented as an example of an S2 activated to solve an S1 (problem situation of indefinite waiting). The watch is an artifact that materializes insights from mathematics, physics, and astronomy but also from design, aesthetics, and psychology.

Thus, it comes across as a cross section of knowledge domains. It has considerable social and affective impact on people – how we organize our lives and how we look or what values we project. The social dimensions and implications become more explicit when we look at the cultural practices the watch introduces, maintains, and transforms. The watch as a timekeeper regulates our working hours, breaks, leisure time, sleep patterns, and appointments. Its importance is intimately linked to maxims such as 'Time is money' and 'Time waits for no one'. Artifacts transform activities and practices, but they also transform the executors of the activity. Before the watch became such an important artifact, people had more relaxed relations with time, duration, intervals, deadlines, and appointments, and some cultures still place less emphasis on such dimensions than others do. Similarly, the word processor has changed our understanding and practices of writing (Heim, 1987) – from a linear, sentence-by-sentence construction of text to a more fluid and multi-focused but potentially fragmented experience of constructing the text and – implicitly – understanding the world. Consequently, the watch, the plowshare, and the word processor embody knowledge domains and influence and potentially transform cultural *practices*. Thus, artifacts suspend the dichotomy between cognition and context; they are mutually constitutive of development.

Artifacts are not necessarily only material. They can be discursive (mastering the lingo of politics and sports or the scientific discourse of quantum physics and relativity theory) or symbolic and semiotic. A prime example is the alphabet. With the relatively few units that make up the semiotic system of the alphabet (representing speech sounds), we can summarize and get access to historically accumulated knowledge or immediate experiences by combining and recombining these units. By the same procedures we can also develop and share new insights – in poetry and plays as well as in research papers and scientific literature. The transformative potential of the alphabet as a cultural artifact is infinite but only when linked to human agency and critical stance.

In discussions and studies of digitalization in education, we argue that artifact is a richer and more precise concept than tool. Artifacts come with the potential of *transforming* the cultures they are introduced into, not by their inherent affordances alone but as a result of the interplay between artifacts and humans' capacity for transformative agency (Arievitch, 2017; Brevik, Gudmundsdottir, Lund, & Strømme, 2019; Haapasaari, Engeström, & Kerosuo, 2014; Sannino, 2015). Artifacts function as gatekeepers to social practices, societies, or cultures (as the plowshare to an agricultural society) and as 'glue' or connective material among those who have appropriated such artifacts as the alphabet (see Chapter 6 for a discussion of appropriation as a concept).

If we apply this line of reasoning to digitalization, we see how computers embody insights developed across a number of domains (mathematics, linguistics, and informatics). In addition, digital resources take on vital affordances connected with artifacts, especially the potential for transforming cultures and cultural practices. For instance, digitalization affords more precise and sophisticated representations of a phenomenon than only the printed text. In the case of math and natural science, we can, by way of models, simulations, animations, and augmented/virtual reality, represent very abstract processes such as hypotheses or dependencies that rest on real-world phenomena or phenomena impossible to study 'live' such as volcano eruptions and earthquakes or phenomena that emerge over generations (e.g., climate change, nutrition patterns). In language and communication domains, machine translation (spoken and written) improves at rapid speed and impacts reading as well as communication practices. In the social sciences, HE benefits by immediate access to infinite information and software that can provide students and staff with overviews of social trends and statistics in a second. However, such information is often fragmented, unverified, contested, and even 'fake', and requires human agents that can synthesize and validate the many diverse sources.

Increasingly, digital artifacts appear as collaborative and communicative partners. Digitalization potentially links minds, hands, and even emotions across time, space, and cultures, but humans are also intimately connected to the resources they activate. In the case of Objects with Intent (OwIs), digital artifacts do not merely reflect the intentions programmed into them (delegated agency), but they can also be "perceived as having need-based agency" (Rozendal et al., p. 25) by their human counterparts, e.g., chatbots or digital/virtual pets used in elderly care. Such partnerships can also take on the shape of dependency, including intimacy and sex in human–robot relationships (Levy, 2007). The presence of 350 million avatars in the world already in 2008 (Facer, 2011) could indicate lasting relationships. For example, Lil Miquela had 1.6 million followers on Instagram in 2019. She is an artist and model for a well-known fashion enterprise. In 2018, people found out that she was an avatar created using computer-generated imagery. The same year *Time* magazine featured her in its '25 Most Influential People on the Internet' lineup. Such development hints at future situations where the boundaries between humans and nonhumans become blurred. The relational and epistemological consequences take us to a pressing concern for HE – the affordances that emerge.

Affordances

Imagine a squirrel climbing a tree. The squirrel's sharp claws enable it to climb the tree, but it could never climb a window. Because of the squirrel claws, the tree represents one type of affordance (positive) for the squirrel, while a windowpane represents another (negative). However, the windowpane and the suction feet of an insect amounts to a positive affordance for the insect. Consequently, the activity of an animal is influenced by the affordance of its body interacting with the environment. Artifacts come with certain inscriptions that make them suitable for certain operations and not others, e.g., keys afford pressing, door knobs afford turning or pressing, and steps afford ascending or descending. The American psychologist James J. Gibson (1979) demonstrated the essence of the term affordance:

> The affordances of the environment are what it offers the animal, what it provides or furnishes, either for good or ill. The verb to afford is found in a dictionary, the noun affordance is not. I have made it up. I mean by it something that refers to both the environment and the animal in a way that no existing term does. It implies the complementary of the animal and the environment.
>
> (p. 127)

When first introduced, Gibson referred to all possible transactions between animals and environments. When applied as an analytical concept in the learning sciences, affordance is often used to refer to possibilities and constraints of things in the environment that humans are aware of – in our context what digitalized learning contexts offer teachers and students. People use cell phones for shopping, podcasting, picturing, networking, studying, etc. (positive affordances), but also for cyberbullying, fraud, fake news, etc. (negative affordances). Similarly, teachers' and students' perceptions of how well digital resources afford their pedagogical and didactic plans will impact how they put them to use. The notion of affordances has played an important role in human–computer interface design, but increasingly also when designing technology-rich educational environments and trajectories (Kennewell, 2001; Lund & Hauge, 2011). In this perspective, the human–artifact relations and the affordances that emerge constitute important principles for designing learning and teaching environments and trajectories (see Chapter 8).

One striking affordance of digitalization is mass collaboration (beyond the small group). In *The Networked Society*, Castells (1996) shows how digitalization has brought about networked structures, configurations, and organizations, perhaps the most powerful and dominant features of 21st-century professional and societal life. When we connect minds, hands, and hearts on a large-scale, potentially infinite, basis, we open up for mass collaboration that can take on complex problems and challenges that have a global character or are too difficult to negotiate for even the most resourceful individual. In the words of professor of world history, Harari (2017), "the crucial factor in our conquest of the world was our ability to connect many humans to one another" (p. 153) and "Sapiens rule the world because they can weave an intersubjective web of meaning" (p. 175).

The prime example of mass collaboration is, of course, Wikipedia, but unbounded collaboration across time, space, and cultures is increasingly found in business models as well as in research and education in and across a plethora of knowledge domains such as health, economics, sustainable development, and climate change (Kaptelinin & Cole, 2002; Lévy, 1997/1999; Lund, 2008; Lund & Rasmussen, 2010). For example, the TakingITGlobal community (https://www.tigweb.org/) advertises that they empower "youth to understand and act on the world's greatest challenges". Another example of such crowdsourcing, but in a more commercial vein, is InnoCentive (https://www.innocentive.com/) advertising online problem-solving by drawing on more than 380,000 problem solvers around the world. Mass collaboration is an affordance made possible because people are embedded in digital environments that allow such collaboration. The actual collaboration causes that digital technologies emerge as resources that extend the cognition of individuals (see Chapter 1). The examples illustrate the dialectic relationship between agents and artifacts, and the affordances that emerge. These are due to the functionalities inscribed in the artifacts by their designers, but also because agents use artifacts in certain ways.

In this chapter, we have sought to demonstrate how cognition and context, mind and available resources are inseparable and situated. Furthermore, we have argued for the value of recognizing digital resources as artifacts, which, depending on peoples' use, come with certain affordances and impact on peoples' epistemic practices (e.g., how phenomena are digitally represented; how communicative spaces emerge; how problem-solving becomes collective, collaborative, and suspending constraints in space and time). This involves conceptual change. From research we know that conceptual change is extremely demanding and requires systematic effort on all levels: institutional, instructional, and student levels, separately as well as multilevel efforts (Vosniadou, 2007). For teachers in HE, it involves more than 'mere' teaching; it involves becoming designers of educational activities, practices, and environments where digital resources are put to use in ways teachers have not been prepared for (Kaptelinin & Nardi, 2006; Lund & Hauge, 2011, see also Chapter 8). This calls for transformative agency (Stetsenko, 2017) or, as Rückriem (2009) argues, digitalization is a fundamentally transformative factor that rests on interagency and networking between humans and also nonhumans. Implicit in such transformation are questions relating to quality issues in HE. These will be discussed in Chapter 3.

References

Arievitch, I. M. (2017). *Beyond the Brain. An Agentive Activity Perspective on Mind, Development and Learning.* Rotterdam, NE: Sense Publishers.

Bates, A. W., & Sangrà, A. (2011). *Managing Technology in Higher Education: Strategies for Transforming Teaching and Learning.* San Francisco, CA: Jossey-Bass.

Brevik, L. M., Gudmundsdottir, G. B., Lund, A., & Strømme, T. A. (2019). Transformative Agency in Teacher Education: Fostering Professional Digital Competence. *Teachers and Teacher Education, 86.* doi: 10.1016/j.tate.2019.07.005

Castells, M. (1996). *The Rise of the Network Society.* Cambridge, MA: Blackwell Publishers.

Conole, G. (2008). The Role of Mediating Artefacts in Learning Design. In L. Lockyer, S. Bennett, S. Agostinho & B. Harper (Eds.), *Handbook of Research on Learning Design and Learning Objects: Issues, Applications, and Technologies* (Vol. 1, pp. 188–207). Hershey, PA: IGI Global.

de Laat, M., Lally, V., Simons, R.-J., & Wenger, E. (2006). A Selective Analysis of Empirical Findings in Networked Learning Research in Higher Education: Questing for Coherence. *Educational Research Review, 1,* 99–111.

Engeström, Y., Miettinen, R., & Punamäki, R. (1999). *Perspectives on Activity Theory.* Cambridge; New York, NY: Cambridge University Press.

Facer, K. (2011). *Learning Futures. Education, Technology and Social Change.* London; New York, NY: Routledge.

Gibson, J. J. (1979). *The Ecological Approach to Visual Perception.* Boston, MA: Houghton Mifflin.

Haapasaari, A., Engeström, Y., & Kerosuo, H. (2014). The Emergence of Learners' Transformative Agency in a Change Laboratory Intervention. *Journal of Education and Work.* doi:10.1080/13639080.2014.900168

Heim, M. (1987). *Electric Language. A Philosophical Study of Word Processing* (2nd ed.). New Haven, CT; London: Yale University Press.

Hutchins, E. (1995). *Cognition in the Wild.* Cambridge, MA: MIT Press.

Kaptelinin, V., & Cole, M. (2002). Individual and Collective Activities in Educational Computer Game Playing. In T. Koschmann, R. Hall & N. Miyake (Eds.), *CSCL2: Carrying Forward the Conversation* (pp. 303–316). Mahwah, NJ; London: Lawrence Erlbaum Associates.

Kaptelinin, V., & Nardi, B. A. (2006). *Acting with Technology: Activity Theory and Interaction Design*. Cambridge, MA; London: MIT Press.

Kennewell, S. (2001). Using Affordances and Constraints to Evaluate the Use of Information and Communications Technologies in Teaching and Learning. *Journal of Information Technology for Teacher Education, 10*(1&2), 101–116.

Koschmann, T. (Ed.). (1996). *CSCL: Theory and Practice of an Emerging Paradigm*. Mahwah, NJ: Lawrence Erlbaum Associates Inc.

Latour, B. (1999). *Pandora's Hope. Essays on the Reality of Science Studies*. Cambridge, MA; London: Harvard University Press.

Levy, D. (2007). *Love + Sex with Robots: The Evolution of Human-Robot Relationships*. New York, NY: Harper.

Lévy, P. (1997/1999). *Collective Intelligence. Mankind's Emerging World in Cyberspace* (R. Bononno, Trans., 1st ed.). Cambridge, MA: Helix Books, Perseus.

Lillejord, S., Børte, K., Nesje, K., & Rud, E. (2018). *Learning and Teaching with Technology in Higher Education – A Systematic Review*. Oslo, NO: Knowledge Centre for Education.

Lund, A. (2008). Wikis: A Collective Approach to Language Production. *ReCALL, 20*(1), 35–54.

Lund, A., & Hauge, T. E. (2011). Designs for Teaching and Learning in Technology Rich Learning Environments. *Nordic Journal of Digital Literacy, 4*, 258–271.

Lund, A., & Rasmussen, I. (2010). Tasks 2.0: Education Meets Social Computing and Mass Collaboration. In C. Crawford, D. A. Willis, R. Carlsen, I. Gibson, K. McFerrin, J. Price & R. Weber (Eds.), *Proceedings of Society for Information Technology & Teacher Education International Conference 2010* (pp. 4058–4065). Chesapeake, VA: AACE.

Orlikowski, W. J., & Iacono, C. S. (2001). Research Commentary: Desperately Seeking the 'IT' in IT Research – A Call to Theorizing the IT Artifact. *Information Systems Research, 12*(2), 121–134.

Rückriem, G. (2009). Digital Technology and Mediation: A Challenge to Activity Theory. In A. Sannino, H. Daniels & K. Gutiérrez (Eds.), *Learning and Expanding with Activity Theory* (pp. 88–111). New York, NY: Cambridge University Press.

Sannino, A. (2015). The Emergence of Transformative Agency and Double Stimulation: Activity-Based Studies in the Vygotskian Tradition. *Learning, Culture, and Social Interaction, 4*, 1–3. doi:10.1016/j.lcsi.2014.07.001

Shaffer, D. W., & Clinton, K. A. (2006). Toolforthoughts: Reexamining Thinking in the Digital Age. *Mind, Culture, and Activity, 13*(4), 283–300.

Stahl, G. (2006). *Group Cognition: Computer Support for Building Collaborative Knowledge*. Cambridge, MA: MIT Press.

Stensaker, B., Maassen, P., Borgan, M., Oftebro, M., & Karseth, B. (2007). Use, Updating and Integration of ICT in Higher Education: Linking Purpose, People and Pedagogy. *Higher Education, 54*, 417–433. doi:10.1007/s10734-006-9004

Strijbos, J. W., Kirschner, P. A., & Martens, R. L. (2004). What We Know About CSCL … and What We Do Not (But Need to) Know about CSCL. In J. W. Strijbos, P. A. Kirschner & R. L. Martens (Eds.), *What We Know about CSCL: And Implementing It in Higher Education* (pp. 245–259). Boston, MA; Dordrecht; New York; London: Kluwer Academic Publishers.

Säljö, R. (1999). Learning as the Use of Tools. A Sociocultural Perspective on the Human-technology Link. In K. Littleton & P. Light (Eds.), *Learning with Computers. Analysing Productive Interaction* (pp. 144–161). New York, NY: Routledge.

Säljö, R. (2010). Digital Tools and Challenges to Institutional Traditions of Learning: Technologies, Social Memory and the Performative Nature of Learning. *Journal of Computer Assisted Learning, 26*(1), 53–64.

Stetsenko, A. (2017). *The Transformative Mind. Expanding Vygotsky's Approach to Development and Education.* New York, NY: Cambridge University Press.

Tegmark, M. (2017). *Life 3.0. Being Human in the Age of Artificial Intelligence.* London: Penguin Random House UK.

Vosniadou, S. (2007). Conceptual Change and Education. *Human Development, 50*(1), 47–54.

Vygotsky, L. S. (1978). *Mind in Society: The Development of Higher Psychological Processes.* Cambridge, MA: Harvard University Press.

Wertsch, J. V. (1998). *Mind as Action.* Oxford: Oxford University Press.

3 Educational quality, transformation, and digitalization

Chapters 1 and 2 provided a rationale and concepts for examining digitalization in HE. We have sought to establish a position from which we approach digitalization through lenses of transformative agency and epistemic practices based on a principled view of digital resources as artifacts that have the potential to help agents break out of status quo and transform (problem) situations they find themselves in.

The elephant

Before we move into the empirical territory to unpack and operationalize the implications of the approaches mentioned above, we need to come to grips with one of the more delicate, complex, and challenging phenomena in educational research – educational quality. Quality is the proverbial elephant in the room; everybody recognizes its presence or absence, but people often avoid talking about it due to vague and often contested definitions.

We turn our interest to the features of the elephant and ask the reader to keep the well-known Indian parable of the blind men and the elephant in mind. As each of the blind men perceived the elephant by feeling a specific body part – trunk, tusk, or tail – they came to conceptualize the entire animal based on limited and subjective experience, disconnected from the equally valid perceptions of others or shared insights (Figure 3.1).

The parable is an excellent metaphor for recognizing quality in HE (and elsewhere) as a *relative* concept – relative to the observer/user and relative to the phenomenon to which it is applied. No wonder Ball (1985) titled his classic essay "What the hell is quality?"

In order to avoid the situation with the blind men, we can fortunately consult scholars who have made valuable contributions to conceptualizing the notoriously fuzzy and subjective idea of what amounts

Figure 3.1 "And so these men of Indostan disputed loud and long, each in his own opinion exceeding stiff and strong, though each was partly in the right and all were in the wrong!".
Source: From the poem "The Blind Men and the Elephant", by John Godfrey Saxe, 1872.

to quality and how it can be recognized. The scholarly literature on quality is massive, and since we do not want to engage in conceptual exegesis, we draw on a highly selected number of relevant studies that offer perspectives on transformation and affordances of digitalization, presented throughout the first two chapters. Let us start by some delimitation. Measuring or assessing quality in terms of 'added value' (Bennett, 2001), expressed in, e.g., reduced retention rates among students, less expense per student or employee, or better grades, will not occupy our focus, although we do acknowledge the need to measure quality in HE. Instead, we establish a line of argument for how we might perceive educational quality in the digital age.

Cluster concepts

Wittek and Kvernbekk (2011) discuss quality as a cluster concept. Their survey of literature shows that quality is understood in widely different ways. The question that arises is whether diverse understandings and usage have anything in common or whether they are strictly 'local' and do not travel beyond the immediate context. The authors do not find any common core or 'essence' attributed to the notion of quality, but investigate how quality is linked to social and ethical significance, i.e., they take a more pragmatic than essentialist approach to the concept. The consequence is accepting a concept as 'vague', with blurred boundaries, borderline cases, and uncertainty. Just as in the well-known thought experiment of which single grain of wheat that transforms a non-heap into a heap, it is futile to identify the single element that transforms the mundane into the excellent. Nevertheless, excellence exists and can be identified. Both quality and transformation emerge as concepts where we instead of an identifiable essence can observe a series of overlapping similarities, a "family of resemblances" (p. 682) that serves to make a cluster concept *function*. No universal definition exists. Instead, cluster concepts such as quality and transformation consist of dimensions that, when combined, form a whole and becomes more powerful than the separate indicators. Thus, the power is in the relations between components. Cluster concepts are used to identify and theorize complex phenomena as quality, but also democracy, family, gaming, etc.

We argue that this excursion into conceptual territory is necessary in order to avoid only measurable quality enhancement and strictly quantitative-driven efforts to prove or disprove that digitalization 'works' or materializes in 'added value'. In line with Vestøl (2015) and Wittek and Kvernbekk (2011), we argue that quantitative indicators often lack contextual information that is necessary to identify quality. For instance, in many subjects teachers identify grade A and separate it from grade B, without quantified indicators. The (often blurred) distinctions between grades are explained qualitatively, in prose, using indicators such as, e.g., independent reasoning and capacity to link local phenomena to global issues.

Quality as transformation

Widely acknowledged as a seminal text on quality, Harvey and Green's "Defining Quality" (1993) relates the concept specifically to HE. The authors identify five categories (for analytic purposes, there are overlaps and subcategories) of quality: quality as exceptional, quality as perfection or consistency, quality as fitness for purpose, quality as value for money, and quality as transformation. The latter category, transformation, holds special interest in the current volume as we pursue the transformative potential of digitalization. Briefly, a transformative view of quality involves qualitative change, physical as well as cognitive. Harvey and Green (1993) assert that "transformation is not unidirectional, a dialectical process is taking place with a negotiated outcome (...) This leads to two notions of quality in education, enhancing the consumer and empowering the consumer" (p. 24). Although we have reservations about the 'consumer' image of the student, we see that the student is firmly at the center of attention when assessing transformative quality in education. This implies that quality is not necessarily recognized unless those who take part in efforts to transform are agentive and, through transformation, becomes empowered. For example, teaching with technology might be 'more fun' because the didactic palette is more diversified, 'more exhilarating' because it involves added risks and uncertainty, and 'more satisfying' because it can involve design and even artistry or intellectual challenge.

There is a clear parallel between a transformative perspective on quality and the principles of double stimulation presented in Chapter 1 – a problem situation (S1) requires transformative agency in order to be resolved. This is an extremely important point as we at this juncture can forge a link between transformative agency, mediating artifacts, and educational quality; agency is enacted when artifacts are appropriated and put to use, and the situation and the agent(s) undergo change. From a pedagogical point of view, it is crucial to connect epistemic change with quality and not merely focus on its force or pervasiveness. However, such connections may also be perceived as a threat to HE institutions maintaining traditions, e.g., where academic staff exercise control over programs and content. Critics of perceiving quality as transformation have also pointed to emotions rather than rationality as drivers for transformation, that the concept is only weakly linked to the more formal and curricular dimensions of education, and that transformation has no end point and escapes materialization (Cheng, 2014). The response must be to establish procedures or indicators that distinguish positive and productive transformation from *any* transformation and where the relationship between quality and transformation is operationalized. Few studies empirically demonstrate this. However, one exception is Cheng's (2014) study of how PhD students and their supervisors perceived the relationship between quality and transformation. We allow some space to pursue Cheng's approach, even if the study is not about digitalization. The reason is that Cheng developed what we recognize as a useful analytical framework for identifying quality as transformation, and this can be extrapolated to projects involving digitalization.

Cheng raised two pertinent research questions:

1   How can quality as transformation be applied to PhD education?
2   How are 'quality' and 'transformation' interrelated at PhD level?
(Cheng, 2014, p. 276)

Sixteen PhD students and 16 supervisors were engaged in semistructured interviews and workshops. As for the first research question, results indicate that the perspectives of quality as transformation could generate a kind of control over academic work. Cheng found that

> most interviewees perceived a danger in using indicators to assess quality because it would make quality appear as outcome, as opposed to an ongoing process to improve oneself (...). This view suggests that quality was perceived as a process rather than as a standard of achievement.
>
> (pp. 281–282)

Still, for this volume, the response to research question 2 is more interesting. Cheng identified five main forms of transformation as quality:

- Intellectual transformation: changed perspectives and development of new ways to solve research problems
- Critical transformation: moving from uncertainty to either positive or negative stance, decision-making, a result of students' reflection and discussion
- Personal transformation: developing attitudes, e.g., increased commitment to studying
- Emotional transformation: from frustration to enjoyment and resolve
- Physical transformation: change in the learning environment, both in a purely material sense and through substituting individual and competitive learning with collaborative approaches

Cheng's study operationalizes quality as transformation in a given context. In the project presented below, we apply this approach to an analysis of a project where transformation is essential.

Another way of approaching quality as transformation is to invoke the collective object of the transformative activity, a cornerstone in cultural–historical activity theory (Engeström, Miettinen, & Punamäki, 1999; Foot, 2002; Kaptelinin, 2005). In Chapter 7, we analyze efforts to transform teacher education to ensure that student teachers are well prepared for work in schools with rich access to digital resources. This effort presupposes a shared understanding among teacher educators of the object to be constructed, developing professional digital competence (PDC) – what it entails and how to go about constructing it. The outcomes of the efforts are affected by several levels, from micro activities in teaching–learning situations but also via commitment on meso levels (department heads, administrators, and academic staff) and from macro-level strategies (institutional and policy levels). Consequently, the object is not a predetermined and fixed entity; it will emerge as diverse, temporary instantiations. These instantiations will, in turn, influence and give shape and direction to the process of object construction.

So far, we have introduced different lenses that can be applied to analyze transformative quality initiatives in HE. In the following, we present an example of a project with potential to strengthen educational quality because of its transformative character. Cheng's quality list is applied to show how it can be used as an analytical framework, provide direction, and make "quality as transformation" a less fuzzy phenomenon.

"What remains unsaid" – a project with transformative qualities

In order to display some of the principles and deliberations we have presented, we turn to a project proposal titled "What Remains Unsaid in Communication" that we (the authors) have evaluated. The pressing challenge the applicants wanted to solve, their problem situation or S1 (see Chapter 1), was as follows: A master's program in mental health should prepare students for professions where they will meet people who have been subjected to sexual abuse, drug addiction, or diseases associated with stigma. Consequently, the master students need to learn to communicate with clients about sensitive or 'taboo' issues. Traditional lectures, seminars, and literature studies had proven to fall short, resulting in students feeling 'lost' in communication about sensitive issues when encountering practicum or work life. Through this project, they attempted to break out of this problem situation and impasse by developing a specific digital resource. Based on real-life cases told by clients, the University College, in collaboration with the clients, develop virtual avatars and scenarios. The scenarios include stops where students would have to make decisions concerning how to proceed and what to say. The interlocutor is a teacher or an avatar programmed for certain character traits, initiatives, and responses. Colors visualize emotions and comment boxes visualize thoughts. The students' communicative strategies can be recorded and replayed for joint discussions. The resources were developed to transform the program; what previously was left unsaid and therefore difficult to 'teach' now became accessible for students and teachers to 'experience'.

The combination of digital resources and educational design (i.e., a series of S2; see Chapter 1) made it possible to break out of a problem situation (S1) that had dogged the master program and transform recurrent stifling situations into opportunities for learning and self-reflection. The situations change, but so will the participants as they become more active, aware of, and sensitive towards their own role. In addition, they become better prepared for the work they will encounter as professionals.

The project proposal is interesting when we relate it to the discussion of quality as transformation. For example, all of Cheng's (2014) five forms of quality (see above) of transformation apply to the proposal:

- Intellectual transformation. The project clearly attempts to change and refine students' perspectives and offer new ways to help them sort out problem situations.
- Critical transformation: Students move from uncertainty towards determination and decision-making as a result of shared interactions, reflection, and discussion.
- Personal transformation: The project design aims to increase students' commitment to engage in difficult or awkward situations with clients.
- Emotional transformation: The project aims to transform students from being insecure and reluctant about how to communicate with clients about difficult social or health issues to developing their professionalism and sense of security.
- Physical transformation: The learning environment offers a blend of human and technological resources, breaks with the previous knowledge delivery model, and promotes a collaborative and artifact-mediated approach to learning and teaching.

By applying Cheng's (2014) categories to the project proposal, we see how quality as transformation can be identified in projects like this. Frequently asked questions connected with digitalization go like, e.g., "Do we learn better with ICT?" and "Can we document better learning outcomes with ICT?". Implicitly, answering with a 'yes' equals proof of quality. The above project shows why such questions often are misplaced: First, their premise is a stable or forever fixed epistemic practice with digital resources as merely add-ons. Second, the unit of analysis is restricted to the artifact, not human activity mediated by artifacts. Third, it lacks a transformative perspective. Breaking away from existing and constraining epistemic practices and developing new ones with greater ecological validity and educational quality are beyond the horizon of such questions.

Connecting the dots: what does the literature say?

Connecting the dots – quality, digitalization, and transformation in HE – seems to have escaped research foci, perhaps because of the conceptual fuzziness involved. In order to examine this impression more systematically, we searched in Oria, a portal to all the material that is available in Norwegian academic and research libraries, including a great extent of electronic material from open sources (Oria includes access to approximately 1,000 weekly updated resources, e.g., journals from Taylor & Francis, Routledge, and Emerald and Sage). The items we used to conduct a search were "Quality" (in title) + "Higher Education" (all fields) + "Digitalization" (all fields). Peer-assessed articles written in English and published within the last ten years were included, and the most relevant texts were listed first. Reading through the titles and abstracts verified our hypothesis that few publications make the connection between the terms so that they amount to a concerted research effort on the interdependence of digitalization and quality recognized as transformation.

The search resulted in some articles about quality in specific digital practices. For example, one examined quality in learning management systems and blended learning interactions (Dias & Diniz, 2013). In addition, several publications described how digitalization can possibly be used to give a broad range of people's access to universities. In these, arguments pertaining to sustaining human rights and giving people affordable educational options were typical (Fischman & Ott, 2018; Vetráková, 2013; Watson, Sörqvist, Keim, & Ramanathan, 2018). As just mentioning "higher education" in the publication was enough to be listed, several articles did not specifically focus on educational issues but on, e.g., environmental issues (Anttila & Jussila, 2018) or quality in different countries such as South Korea (Park, 2009), Hong Kong (Sing, 2009), and Japan (Inoguchi & Fujii, 2009).

However, we found the article "Changing tires in the express lane" (Dew, Beitel, & Hare, 2018) highly relevant. In this, three academics with considerable experience in quality work from both industry and education wrote about how digitalization transforms industries and society and triggers a tremendous pressure for change in education – from K–12 to HE. They introduced the concept *Quality 4.0*, which addresses how technology aligns quality with the digital transformation of management systems in order to improve culture, collaboration, competency, and leadership. The challenge, then, is to promote "workforce-development professionals" (p. 32). In the following, we present this contribution in some detail as it also points towards a chain of quality, which we discuss at the end of the chapter.

It is obvious that people would never measure the quality of a bike by comparing it with a car, even if we use both to transport ourselves. Imagine complaints about the bike having two wheels because the car has four. Similarly, Dew et al. (2018) argue that the quality of HE institutions is highly complicated to measure by comparing different institutions based on quantitative surveys. The many attempts to measure quality, often based on quantitative results used to compare HE institutions, undergo critical examination in their article. Purely quantitative approaches do not take into account that HE institutions have different mandates and responsibilities. Some institutions clearly prepare for a high-quality workforce, e.g., law schools, departments of nursing science, and teacher education institutions. Others have undergraduate certificate programs. Regional universities, national universities, and online universities exist, funded by states, student enlistment, or even religious denominations. This diversity calls for quality work and perspectives that embrace the fact that different educations have different purposes and work under different conditions. Therefore, quality work needs to be context specific and relate to whether the institutions' digitalization strategies match their educational purpose. For education, the message is clear: "Too many efforts are only random acts of improvement" (Dew et al., 2018, p. 37). Educators cannot pull off the road to put their educational systems or institutions into the shop for renewal; quality enhancement methods must be implemented, while educational systems and institutions are in motion, "Just as other sectors have done" (p. 38).

To link transformation to quality enhancement, Dew et al. (2018) suggest that educational institutions need a system-wide reliable approach to continuous quality improvement. First, agents from different educational levels must be involved. Second, they argue why students should be partners and not considered merely customers in the process of transforming education: students more than academics have an 'emic' (understood from within) experience of educational activities that promote meaningful learning. The authors suggest developing learning communities of quality workers from different levels of the educational system whose task is to balance between protecting and maintaining practices and systems that work while identifying when and how to transform those that work less well. In Table 3.1, they present a plan–do–study–act (PDSA) model that can be used as a framework for such a community.

Table 3.1 Six steps to educational improvement

PLAN	Validate the need for improvement Baseline results *How are we doing? How do we know?*
	Clarify purpose, goals, and measures Systems alignment *Why are we here?* *What do we need to do well together?* *How will we know how we are doing?*
DO	Adopt and deploy an approach to continual improvement Systems integration *How will we work together to get better?*
	Translate the approach into aligned action PDSA of operations *What will we do differently?*
STUDY	Analyze the results Study trend against baseline data *What happened?*
ACT	Make improvements Adjust operations *What did we do with what we learned?*
	Repeat the cycle

Source: From Drew et al., 2018, p. 35. Reproduced with the kind permission of © Jim Shipley & Associates.

With the PDSA model, we have moved from connecting quality to transformation of epistemic practices to quality as organizational and institutional transformation. The model aims to structure educational transformation as a complex, continuous, and iterative process. Quality workers "realize that they have to work within complex systems, where subsystems co-vary and impact one another in unpredictable ways; they also understand that improvements happen project by project" (p. 32). In the following, we elaborate on the term 'quality work' and link it to transformation and management.

Quality work involving a chain of agents

We have seen how Dew et al. (2018) argue for establishing communities of quality by engaging agents from different levels of the educational system. Their study indicates that quality emerges partly as a result of collaborative culture, partly as legitimate and relevant management. However, Elken and Stensaker (2018) argued that there is a 'missing link' between quality *management*, focusing on internal quality development, leadership, rules, procedures and accounts, and quality *culture*, focusing on collective and distributed commitment to quality. This missing link was named *quality work*, located at the level of situated and contextual practices. Quality work "stands in a dialectical and dynamic relationship to both managerial and cultural perspectives" (p. 4), "stressing the role of actors and their agency in institutions" and with key elements such as "agency, change, intentionality, effort and a processual view on *multiple* practices of quality work" (p. 5, emphasis in original). This view resonates with the view we have attributed to digitalization – how it involves transformative agency and epistemic practices.

Quality as transformation implies an orientation towards an object that is more sophisticated than its current state, more socially and environmentally valid, located at the level of actors and practices but embedded in the norms of local institutions as well as national policies, international trends, and research within the learning sciences. Developing information exchange systems from smoke signals to the Internet is a prime example. However, there is no guarantee of success issued with such efforts. No predetermined outcome can be stated when we engage in transformative and risk-infused endeavors, and failed attempts can bring about valuable insights. Consequently, transformation as quality is constructed, not given.

Scholarly literature reveals that not many studies connect educational quality, transformation, and digitalization. As highlighted in Chapter 1, digitalization understood in this way also seems to have escaped institutional leadership in HE. We use the term 'leadership' in accordance with researchers and theorists who have developed a view of leadership as *distributed* (Gronn, 2008; Hutchins, 1995; Spillane, 2006). Distributed leadership emerged as a reaction to the hierarchical and top-down models of leadership with the individual manager on top, especially in educational contexts. Distributed leadership is highly situated and involves a multiagent perspective; members of the organization exert influence and are not merely executors of decisions from above. The approach recognizes and examines how leadership is distributed among people and resources in the context of a complex organization. The roles of the agents in an organization may change from one situation to another, making leadership a flexible organizational principle.

More systematic excursions into the literature on distributed and transformative leadership reveal few, if any, studies that connect these types of leadership to digitalization (except some in the field of business management). With this as a backdrop, we turn to *the chain of quality* as formulated by Fossland and Ramberg (2016): "We introduce the notion of 'the chain of quality in higher education' to emphasize that developing educational quality requires collaboration between a series of agents at different levels in a 'chain' where there must be quality at all levels" (p. i). The authors identify three main levels: a macro level with national and international agents and policies, a meso level located at the educational institutions and their leaders, and a micro level where we find the agents engaged in colocated and virtual learning environments. In this perspective, horizontal interaction at each level and vertical interaction between the various levels are what constitutes the core of educational quality.

This tall order requires strategies and action plans. The authors conclude that educational leadership is the hub, but this meso level depends on the involvement of the other two. This is where we argue that educational leadership cannot be understood in generic terms but need to draw on insights from distributed leadership. If not, digitalization of educational practices risks being the responsibility and developmental work carried by individual 'beacons' and enthusiasts. Cheng's (2014) five main forms of transformation, cultural–historical activity theory's notion of the object and more sophisticated activity systems, as well as the PDSA model of Dew et al. (2018) connect quality work between agents to larger institutional efforts. In this configuration, we find a framework that HE might use to discuss, initiate, and evaluate transformative initiatives.

It's elephants all the way down!

In this chapter, we have sought to establish an understanding of what educational quality entails and at several levels. In scholarly literature, there are very few connections to be found between notions of educational quality, transformation, and digitalization, and the role of leadership is often absent from a discussion on such connections (see also Chapter 4 and our analysis of a White Paper case). Thus, quality in this context often escapes a solid basis or perceptible indicators, hence our emphasis on Cheng's (2014) study. When seeking to unpack educational quality in digital practices, it is like opening Chinese boxes – a system of nested terms that combine quality with digitalization, transformation, and leadership that is reminiscent of the blind men trying to determine the totality of an elephant by focusing on one aspect. However, it is also an experience of *infinite regress*. This principle alludes to the myth about the world, thinking that a turtle carries it on its back. When being asked what carries the turtle, the answer is that an even bigger turtle underneath rests on an even bigger turtle and so on *ad infinitum*, hence the maxim "It's turtles all the way down". In other versions, the turtle is replaced by an elephant. Regardless of the animal, the myth illustrates the futility of claiming to know the absolute truth, whether it pertains to explain the meaning of life or the meaning of quality: it's elephants all the way down. Still, we believe in developing valid descriptors of and relations between elephants involved.

References

Anttila, J., & Jussila, K. (2018). Universities and Smart Cities: The Challenges to High Quality. *Total Quality Management & Business Excellence, 29*(9–10), 1058–1073. doi:10.1080/14783363.2018.1486552

Ball, C. (1985). What the Hell Is Quality? In C. Ball & D. Urwin (Eds.), *Fitness for Purpose: Essays in Higher Education* (pp. 96–102). Guildford: Society for Research into Higher Education & NFER-Nelson.

Bennett, D. C. (2001). Assessing Quality in Higher Education. *Association of American Colleges and Universities, 87*(2), 1–6.

Cheng, M. (2014). Quality as Transformation: Educational Metamorphosis. *Quality in Higher Education, 20*(3), 272–289. doi:10.1080/13538322.2014.978135

Dew, J., Beitel, A., & Hare, G. (2018). Changing Tires in the Express Lane. *The Journal for Quality and Participation, 40*(4), 31–38.

Dias, S. B., & Diniz, J. A. (2013). FuzzyQoImodel: A Fuzzy Logic-based Modelling of Users' Quality of Interaction with a Learning Management System Under Blended Learning. *Computers & Education, 69*, 38–59. doi:10.1016/j.compedu.2013.06.016

Elken, M., & Stensaker, B. (2018). Conceptualising 'Quality Work' in Higher Education. *Quality in Higher Education*, 1–14. doi:10.1080/13538322.2018.1554782

Engeström, Y., Miettinen, R., & Punamäki, R. (1999). *Perspectives on Activity Theory*. Cambridge; New York, NY: Cambridge University Press.

Fischman, G. E., & Ott, M. (2018). Access, Equity and Quality Trends in Latin America's Public Universities. *International Journal of Educational Development, 58*, 86–94. doi:10.1016/j.ijedudev.2016.11.002

Foot, K. A. (2002). Pursuing an Evolving Object: A Case Study in Object Formation and Identification. *Mind, Culture and Activity, 9*(2), 132–149.

Harvey, L., & Green, D. (1993). Defining Quality. *Assessment & Evaluation in Higher Education, 18*(1), 9–34.

Inoguchi, T., & Fujii, S. (2009). The Quality of Life in Japan. *Social Indicators Research, 92*(2), 227–262. doi:10.1007/s11205-008-9351-3

Kaptelinin, V. (2005). The Object of Activity: Making Sense of the Sense-Maker. *Mind, Culture and Activity, 12*(1), 4–18.

Park, C.-M. (2009). The Quality of Life in South Korea. *Social Indicators Research, 92*(2), 263–294. doi:10.1007/s11205-008-9348-y

Sing, M. (2009). The Quality of Life in Hong Kong. *Social Indicators Research, 92*(2), 295–335. doi:10.1007/s11205-008-9349-x

Vetráková, M. (2013). Quality and Availability of Higher Education at Matej Bel University in Banska Bystrica. *Technologia Vzdelavania, 21*(2), 1–8.

Watson, G., Sörqvist, L., Keim, E., & Ramanathan, N. (2018). Quality Confronts Global Challenges of the Coming Century. *The Journal for Quality and Participation, 40*(4), 4–10.

Wittek, L., & Kvernbekk, T. (2011). On the Problems of Asking for a Definition of Quality in Education. *Scandinavian Journal of Educational Research, 55*(6), 671–684.

4 Digitalization, quality, and policy
The case of a White Paper

Introducing case

In this chapter, we will identify to what extent and how agents from meso and macro levels of Norwegian HE connect digitalization and educational quality. In addition, we investigate and discuss how the means they suggest forge links between digitalization and quality. The backdrop is found in Norway's Ministry of Education and Research inviting institutions and communities to contribute to a White Paper on quality in education.

Across Europe, educators, researchers, and policymakers discuss how HE can realize the potential of digitalization and prepare students for a digitalized working life. There is a plethora of reports and White Papers testifying to such concerns (see, e.g., Alexander, Grajek, & Grama, 2017; Ehlers & Kellermann, 2019; OECD, 2018). Since Norwegian people have ample access to digital technology (in 2019, 98 per cent of Norwegians age 9–69 have access to computers and the internet), the push to take advantage of digital technology for educational challenges is very much articulated. This gives reason to believe that the themes discussed in a Norwegian context are also recognized across Western countries and probably beyond, although local contexts are crucial. Thus, although we would argue that findings may be analytically generalizable, but the reader must consider to what extent they are representative in other contexts.

The missing links

In the previous chapters, we have presented some theoretical and philosophical considerations about digitalization, epistemology, and quality in HE. Our interest in writing these chapters is particularly motivated by years of experience with HE quality work. For many years, we have observed that discussions about digitalization and quality often lack a professional language and are characterized by arguments for or against digitalization and change. In addition, links between digitalization and quality are rarely articulated. Our intention with the previous chapters has been not only to raise issues of digitalization, transformation, and quality but also to promote a professional language that might benefit discussions about HE quality in a digital age.

Transforming educational practices seems difficult. For instance, a systematic review (Lillejord, Børte, Nesje, & Ruud, 2018) shows that implementing digital resources to enhance student active learning takes time and concludes that digital resources more frequently are used for administrative than educational purposes. The authors highlight that an institutionally led strategic process towards transformation is lacking. Consequently, transformation has been *ad hoc* or randomly introduced and administered.

Nevertheless, decades with access to digital artifacts in education and individual teachers' efforts to explore the potential of digitalization in their practices have resulted in an accumulation of experiences of educational value, e.g., collaboration, student active learning, engagement, creativity, and learning processes that have validity for working life. Even if findings are often based on case studies and interventions at the micro level, they are of considerable educational interest when juxtaposing such studies indicates that certain digital practices can stimulate productive learning processes, while others might be counterproductive. Findings also indicate that institutional leadership of digitalization is lacking. The trend has been that individual teachers are "drivers" of development but without sufficient strategic support.

This trend is not new. Already in 1976, Weick (1976) in his seminal paper made an effort to understand why educational institutions are so stable and difficult to change. One reason, he argued, was what he called a "loosely coupled system" where employees largely work individually. Such a system typically has broad individual freedom and weak structures for collective institutional development. Another explanation might be that teaching and learning practices in many programs and subjects have deep historical roots in practices that have stood the test of time, and therefore are hard to change even when times change dramatically (Olson, 2003).

To sum up, discussions about digitalization and quality often lack a professional language. Second, we see that several micro-level studies indicate that certain uses of digital practices are valuable for student learning, but that digitalization in education also involves risks. Third, clearer leadership of digitalization in HE is often articulated as recommendation; the individual beacon at micro level is not sufficient. In 2015, Damşa et al. showed that there is a need for more studies on quality work and "the linkages between external and structural framework conditions, how universities and colleges govern their educational responsibilities and quality enhancement at micro level" (p. 64).

We suggest that the missing link is how HE institutions (HEIs; meso level) and governments (macro level) systematically relate digitalization to educational quality. In 2016, we were given the opportunity to further pursue and explore such a link in an analysis of the connections between digitalization and educational quality in Norwegian HE (Aagaard, Lund, Lanestedt, Ramberg, & Swanberg, 2018). In the following, we also connect this study to the larger issues of the current volume in order to add empirical dimensions to our reasoning.

In 2016, the Norwegian Ministry of Education and Research invited universities, university colleges, and other relevant actors to submit contributions while preparing White Paper 16 (2016–2017) on Quality Culture in Higher Education. In his invitation, the Minister presented the following characteristics of educational quality:

1   Ambitions on behalf of students
2   Active and varied learning activities
3   Quality culture and clear education management
4   Integration of students in the academic community
5   Interaction between Universities and University Colleges and private enterprise

The Minister did not explicitly ask for perspectives on the role of digitalization in promoting education quality. Still, the documents indirectly provided insights into connections between quality and digitalization at both meso and macro levels. To demonstrate this, we conducted a content analysis (Braun & Clarke, 2006; Clarke & Braun, 2014) of 21 written responses to the Ministry's White Paper in order to answer the following question:

1   To what extent and how are educational quality and digitalization connected and described?
2   Which means are suggested to enhance digitalization and educational quality?

Method

We analyzed 22 of 91 submissions from the groups shown in Table 4.1:

The sample mainly consists of submissions from large and small universities and university colleges, but also two student organizations, four interest organizations, and four national players (e.g., the Norwegian Research Council and the National Agency for Quality in Education). We included universities and university colleges that are geographically dispersed, have different special fields, and together represent a large and diverse proportion of HE students in Norway. Most Norwegian HE is governmental and free, but one private institution was included. Analytically, we sought a representative sample (Yin, 2010) but without aiming for statistically generalized findings.

After selecting documents, we conducted a thematic analysis (Braun & Clarke, 2006; Clarke & Braun, 2014) to identify, analyze, and report patterns (themes) within the data. A "pattern" or "theme" intends to capture what seems important in the data in light of the research questions. Thus, we focused on patterns of meaning in the data corpus, partly guided by predefined questions and partly through discursive manifestations of the topic that we had decided to look for.

We identified statements about digitalization and quality, e.g., descriptions about what HE does to ensure that digitization promotes educational quality. Further, we analyzed reasons and purposes for promoting the extended use of digital resources, and challenges HE faces and where HE places responsibility for digital development (with educational policymakers, within HE itself on an institutional level, or in micro practices enacted by the academic staff). Since patterns may also emerge at a more latent level, we analyzed the data corpus a second time in order to uncover patterns or indications we might have overlooked the first time.

Applying thematic identification principles guided the analysis. The combination of what interested us as researchers and characteristics of the data was in the foreground. Six researchers and one student were involved, testing interpretations and discussing patterns in the data. Hence, we strove for conceptual validity (Mishler, 1990) and that the

Table 4.1 Sample

Universities	University colleges	Student organizations	Interest organizations	National players	Total
8	4	2	4	4	22

topics we identified should be distinct, coherent, and consistent. We distributed the contributions from the HEIs and other actors between three groups who first read and charted the patterns that we found at semantic level, using categories that corresponded to our research questions. We then wrote syntheses using a coauthoring tool. Quotes were included to provide empirical support to the syntheses. The chart gave an overview and foundation for discussing and identifying latent topics across the contributions. After analyzing the submissions, we did a semantic analysis of agreement and variety between descriptions in the contributions and the White Paper, again guided by the research questions.

In the following, we present the topics and highlight similarities and differences as to how relations between digitalization and educational quality were described and discussed in the submitted HE contributions and the White Paper.

Findings

Digitalization and educational quality

The semantic analysis showed that all submitted contributions except one connected digitalization to educational quality. Although it varied how explicit and clear the authors described the connection, they mentioned similar reasons why digitalization in HE is a good thing: digital resources can be used to promote job relevance, make education flexibly available for students on as well as across campuses, and enhance student-active learning. Several contributions stated that when work life requires high digital competence, students must develop such competence during their studies. Some added that HE must adjust or change traditional didactics and assessment practices to appear as work relevant. However, very few analyzed or described what professional digital competence (PDC) implied or exemplified how students can develop such a competence. Most descriptions were vague and stopped by inserting adjectives such as "student-active", "innovative", and "experimental". Nevertheless, digitalization was clearly associated with work relevance across the total data corpus.

In addition, it was typically mentioned that digitalization makes it possible to coordinate programs or subjects across campuses and make them available to more students. The students also very clearly suggested that HE should use more dissemination and communication technologies to make education more available to everyone.

The White Paper (Ministry of Education and Research, 2017) states that digitalization creates new conditions and opportunities for teaching and learning and new ways of communicating and organizing. It also makes explicit that all students are expected to meet activating and varied forms of learning and assessment, utilizing digital opportunities, and various examples of digitized practices, including exams. This is central to developing critical thinking, reflection, collaborative competence, etc. Nevertheless, the Ministry emphasizes, it seems as if digital resources often are more successful in managing and supervising learning than in supporting the actual learning processes and that professional staff does little to connect the use of digital tools to the curricula, subject descriptions, and work requirements. This echoes findings in the international literature we referred to at the opening of Chapter 1.

How are educational quality and digitalization connected and described?

As mentioned previously, the submitted contributions from the invited institutions and bodies typically contain vague and general descriptions of connections between digitalization and educational quality. Instead of referring to research when they argue why digital technology should be used more often in learning and teaching, they usually refer to policy documents. In addition, we found that the data corpus contains very few reflections about how digitalization changes learning and knowledge practices. Only two mention the importance of understanding the connections between digitally competent students and how they learn when digital resources are mobilized. As already argued in Chapter 1, how we get to, maintain, and develop knowledge in digital and web-based environments and across multiple contexts is an important issue for HE (see also Ludvigsen, Lund, Rasmussen, & Säljö, 2010). In light of this, the absence of such reflections is worth pondering.

One of the clearest distinctions between the contributions and the White Paper itself is the perspectives on learning, technology, and knowledge. While fundamental epistemological perspectives are rarely expressed in the contributions, the White Paper starts with the following headline: "Preface – knowledge is developed in collaboration" – a clear-cut epistemological position. Further, reflections about the epistemological implications of digitalization emerge in paragraphs like this:

> The use of digital technology leads to changes in just about every area of the modern society and has, in a short time, reversed the rules of the game in different industries. What digitalization

implies for higher education, we have just begun to see the contours of (Bowen 2015; NOU 2014: 5) (...) Our everyday lives are increasingly controlled by algorithms and data, and this affects the way we make decisions (O'Neill 2016). (...) The students must be able to reflect on ethical, legal and security issues concerning use of data and technology. They must be able to ask new critical questions (...).

(p. 12)

Consequently, the Ministry of Education and Research presents a view on learning that coincides with what is our point of departure in this book. The White Paper refers to research literature and recognizes digital resources as artifacts with intentions that are "written into" them and emphasizes that they affect our social practices. Further, the White Paper suggests that digital technologies can transform and exceed established educational practices but also influence the content HEIs need to focus on (e.g., ethical and security issues). Thus, what we see in the White Paper is an instance of research and policy development converging, an amalgamation not necessarily confined to a Norwegian context.

Means to enhance digitalization and educational quality

The HE contributions submitted to the White Paper suggest that there are major differences between HEIs when it comes to digitalization. A small number of universities leave the impression that they are on the forefront of linking digitalization and educational quality, while most admit that there is a long way to go before taking proper advantage of digital resources in HE. Even if most describe digitalization in education as the universities' or university colleges' responsibility, many also ask for national support to develop practices as well as organization. Generally, most submitted contributions request a sharing culture and national meeting places to discuss and share lessons learned from pedagogical innovations.

A typical statement is that faculty staff need to develop their pedagogical competence in general and their knowledge about digitalization and learning in particular. However, the analyzed inputs leave the impression that education is still living in the "shadow of research" and that a nationally coordinated action is required to solve this problem. In general, most state that it is a national responsibility to establish incentives and merit systems to stimulate the academic staff into developing innovative teaching practices more aligned with how we engage in epistemic work outside HEIs.

Management

The contributions only rarely mention the importance of educational management. Exploring the educational value of using digital resources still seems to rely on teachers' practices at micro level, i.e., interactions, designs, and enactment of activities. The authors of the HE contributions do not highlight the importance of leaders, but instead ask for national governance (macro level) and incentives that will promote local quality enhancing initiatives. In contrast, the White Paper presents two chapters on governance and management. It is expected that the boards and management levels of HE "prioritize the quality of education in the distribution of resources, strategies and communication, and that they communicate these priorities to the entire organization" (Ministry of Education and Research, 2017, p. 83, our translation). Institution and study program management should facilitate "that the entire academic community, and not just enthusiasts, use the opportunities digitalization provides to raise the quality of education" and "that the institutions will lift the development of digital solutions to a strategic level and define goals and measures for digitizing learning processes" (p. 69, our translation). The quotes amount to concerns and expectations from policy level to HEIs, while the HEIs articulate a need for support from policy level in order to meet these. National arenas emerge as a prime candidate for collective efforts and collaboration and overcoming the 're-inventing the wheel' syndrome.

So what?

This book is highly motivated by what we have observed as weak theoretical and research-based discussions about digitalization and educational quality. This is worrying when considering our White Paper case that shows how digital development seems to be pushed by policymakers. It is therefore interesting and, to some extent, surprising as well as inspiring to see how policymakers authoring the final version of the White Paper support their arguments by referring to research and that it contains reflections about epistemological consequences of digitalization.

In 2015, Damsa and colleagues argued that we need more studies on "quality work" – analysis of the linkages between how universities and colleges govern their educational responsibilities, and quality enhancement work at micro level. While such multilevel analysis and knowledge is theoretically interesting, it could also provide policymakers with new insights into how state funding is spent most effectively

(Damşa et al., 2015, p. 64). However, our findings indicate that HE also needs more knowledge about the studies that already exist. After decades of introducing digital technologies in HE, researchers have studied some of their educational potentials and constraints as well as the challenges that emerge in technology-rich learning environments. In Chapter 5, we present what we found in our effort to get an updated overview of such research and to what extent the researchers highlight the same potential as the authors of the contributions: to promote work relevance, coordinate, and offer programs and studies across campuses and make them readily and flexibly available to students.

The HE sector is in the middle of an extremely interesting and demanding time of change, and will need further knowledge about how responsibility can be distributed between educational authorities, institutional and interactional levels. Digitalization has triggered society and most industries to change. This has led to an exponential increase in digital development over the past 50 years, which only seems to continue. This goes especially for artificial intelligence, data mining, and virtual realities. This is one of the reasons why we in Chapter 3 have argued for looking at "quality as transformation" in a digital age; epistemic work with and without digital resources amounts to very different outcomes (Harari, 2017; Säljö, 2010). However, we have also argued that pedagogical and didactical practices in HE seem challenging to transform (Dew, Beitel, & Hare, 2018). The analysis shows that this still seems to be the case. We will therefore pursue this issue and discuss how transformation in HE can be initiated, appropriated, and sustained.

As mentioned in Chapter 3, Fossland and Ramberg (2016) suggest that if agents from both the national and international levels (macro level), leaders of HE (meso level) as well as teachers and students in classrooms (micro level) jointly engage in transforming (the so-called chain of quality), digitalization will have better chances of succeeding. In recent years, European governments and HEIs have shown increased interest in the quality and excellence of teaching and learning and in developing aims, measures, and indicators to achieve high-quality teaching (Kottmann, Huisman, Mampaey, Brockerhoff, & Cremonini, 2016). The analyzed White Paper is an example. Also the European Commission's High Level Group (McAleese et al., 2013) states that new and emerging technologies are starting to transform HE and add that "there is every reason to harness the potential of these developments in the service of high quality higher education" (p. 14). However, policymakers can only provide institutions with frameworks and guidelines. A Norwegian national survey from 2015 showed that 79 per cent of leaders in Norwegian HE thought that the individual teacher should decide whether digital tools should be used in their subjects or not. In our introduction to this chapter, we presented several studies that critically questioned what seems like a random implementation of digital technologies in HE. Our findings indicate that HEIs still lack a focus on the connection between digitalization, pedagogy, and educational quality. Leaders of HE have decisive influence on quality work and are responsible for creating productive, local frameworks and an institutional learning culture that includes the teachers. In light of this, it is remarkable that management perspectives are almost absent in the contributions but highlighted in two chapters in the White Paper.

Management is an interesting discussion when transforming HE is the objective. We need to be reminded that HE is a loosely coupled system with strong historical roots that make it challenging to take on deep transformation and not merely superficial change. However, challenges can trigger development. Friction forces "creation of knowledge, which not only pertains to coordinating pieces of knowledge, but also moulding them together into new forms" (Hoholm, 2011, p. 19). Cultural–historical perspectives on learning suggest exploring challenges and tensions emerging when traditional ways of educating students do not work anymore and questions arise as to how it might be conducive to transform the existing activity system into a more sophisticated one: What is happening? Why change? In which direction? For what purposes? How? Furthermore, teachers need structures that support them in complex and demanding situations when views that are taken for granted are questioned, and they are pushed towards their 'edge of competence'. The likelihood of mastering a potentially transformative situation increases if professional networks are established. Networks are better than individuals' in finding ways out of dilemmas, conflicts, or double binds that typically emerge in such phases (Engeström, 1987; Fenwick & Edwards, 2014). Managing transformation and innovative processes therefore seems to be the equivalent of navigating and building networks, rather than merely exercising control.

In both contributions to and the final version of the White Paper, it is argued that academic staff needs to explore new teaching and learning strategies. This is supported by the fact that several of the institutions giving input to the White Paper have established teaching and learning centers (TLCs) to promote educational quality across disciplines and programs, often with a connection to digitalized practices. The mandate of such centers is typically to promote educational quality by supporting teachers' development of pedagogical, didactic, and digital competencies. Establishing TLCs is also an international trend (see, e.g., Holt, Palmer, & Challis, 2011). However, they seem to be differently organized. Some have an administrative character, others a more digitally oriented character, while some aim to foster "hybrid competencies" by juxtaposing and merging, e.g., media, technological, and pedagogical competencies in the academic community in question.

Developing HE quality involves transforming and even innovating pedagogical practices. Innovation always carries a degree of uncertainty and implies that uncertainty is reduced (although not removed) by learning from and building on experience and continuous feedback (Hoholm, 2011). According to Pavitt (2005), only two aspects of the innovation process are generic, "coordinating and integrating specialized knowledge, and learning under conditions of uncertainty" (p. 109). Hence, the management of uncertainty is one of the crucial tasks for participants in such processes. There are indications that TLCs that integrate diverse and specialized knowledge by engaging people from different subject domains will be better prepared to manage risks and uncertainty (Lund & Eriksen, 2016). By stimulating faculty staff with complementary competencies to discuss or "investigate" the questions and tensions mentioned above, it will also be possible to push colleagues to their edge of competence and possibly exceed the single competence by connecting the many (Holt, Palmer & Challis, 2011).

In the introduction to this chapter, we pointed to the fact that educational traditions and some subject specific traditions have resilient historical roots; even when contexts change, practices tend to remain stable (Olson, 2003). However, an 'outsider' might more easily than an 'insider' be able to identify and question traditions, and find ways to reduce uncertainty through critical and creative discussions. Therefore, TLCs with hybrid competencies seem well prepared to take responsibility for educational quality work and prevent digitalization from merely becoming (or remaining) an administrative and instrumental task (see also Hakkarainen, Palonen, Paavola, & Lehtinen, 2004).

Apart from the emergence of TLCs, developing pedagogical courses and providing incentives that motivate faculty staff to engage in transformative and innovative practices, including risks and uncertainty, also seem a relevant means. Within Norway and across Europe, very different pedagogical course designs are offered and developed (Lillejord et al., 2018). The diversity of courses that emerge can therefore give valuable insights into characteristics of course designs that promote educational quality. Different standards and demands for employees' formal pedagogical competence can also generate challenges, e.g., when teachers change jobs from one university to another. One fairly detailed unpacking of a case (the White paper experience) can perhaps be analytically generalized, but is of local character and may not be empirically valid beyond the context. Therefore, in Chapter 5, we turn our attention to what research can tell us about the affordances that digital technologies have in HE and how these are appropriated.

References

Aagaard, T., Lund, A., Lanestedt, J., Ramberg, K. R., & Swanberg, A. B. (2018). Sammenhenger mellom digitalisering og utdanningskvalitet–innspill og utspill. *Uniped, 41*(3), 289–303.

Alexander, B., Grajek, S., & Grama, J. L. (2017). Trend Watch 2017: Which IT Trends Is Higher Education Responding To? Research Report: *EDUCAUSE*.

Damşa, C., de Lange, T., Elken, M., Esterhazy, R., Fossland, T., Frølich, N., ... Nordkvelle, Y. T. (2015). *Quality in Norwegian Higher Education: A Review of Research on Aspects Affecting Student Learning*. Oslo: NIFU.

Dew, J., Beitel, A., & Hare, G. (2018). Changing Tires in the Express Lane. *The Journal for Quality and Participation, 40*(4), 31–38.

Ehlers, U.-D., & Kellermann, S. A. (2019). *Future Skills. The Future of Learning and Higher Education* (pp. 2–69). Karlsruhe, DE: nextskills.org.

Engeström, Y. (1987). *Learning by Expanding: An Activity – Theoretical Approach to Developmental Research*. Helsinki: Orienta-konsultit.

European Commission High Level Group (2015). *Standards and Guidelines for Quality Assurance in the European Higher Education Area (ESG)*. Brussels, Belgium.

Fenwick, T., & Edwards, R. (2014). Networks of Knowledge, Matters of Learning, and Criticality in Higher Education. *Higher Education, 67*(1), 35–50. doi:10.1007/s10734-013-9639-3

Fossland, T., & Ramberg, K. R. (2016). *Kvalitetskjeden i høyere utdanning – en guide for digital kompetanse og undervisningskvalitet*. ISBN 978-82-91308-57-9. Norgesuniversitetets skriftserie (1/2016).

Hakkarainen, K., Palonen, T., Paavola, S., & Lehtinen, E. (2004). *Communities of Networked Expertise*. Amsterdam: Elsevier/Earli.

Harari, Y. N. (2017). *Homo Deus*. London: Vintage.

Hoholm, T. (2011). *Contrary Forces of Innovation: An Ethnography of Innovation in the Food Industry*. London: Palgrave Macmillan.

Holt, D., Palmer, S., & Challis, D. (2011). Changing Perspectives: Teaching and Learning Centres' Strategic Contributions to Academic Development in Australian Higher Education. *International Journal for Academic Development, 16*(1), 5–17.

Kottmann, A., Huisman, J., Mampaey, J., Brockerhoff, L., & Cremonini, L. (2016). *How Can One Create a Culture for Quality Enhancement? Final report. CHEPS, CHEGG.*

Lillejord, S., Børte, K., Nesje, K., & Ruud, E. (2018). *Learning and Teaching with Technology in Higher Education – A Systematic Review.* Oslo: Knowledge Center for Education.

Ludvigsen, S. R., Lund, A., Rasmussen, I., & Säljö, R. (2010). *Learning across Sites: New Tools, Infrastructures and Practices.* Oxon, UK: Routledge.

Lund, A., & Eriksen, T. M. (2016). Teacher Education as Transformation: Some Lessons Learned from a Center for Excellence in Education. *Acta Didactica Norge, 10*(2), 53–72.

McAleese, M., Bladh, A., Berger, V., Bode, C., Muehlfeit, J., Petrin, T., ... & Tsoukalis, L. (2013). High Level Group on the Modernisation of Higher Education. *Report to the European commission on improving the quality of teaching and learning in Europe's higher education institutions.*

Ministry of Education and Research (2017). *Meld. St. 16 (2016–2017). Quality Culture in Higher Education.* Oslo: Government.

Mishler, E. (1990). Validation in Inquiry-guided Research: The Role of Exemplars in Narrative Studies. *Harvard Educational Review, 60*(4), 415–443.

OECD (2018). *OECD Science, Technology and Innovation Outlook 2018.* Adapting to Technological and Societal Disruption. Paris: OECD.

Olson, D. R. (2003). *Psychological Theory and Educational Reform. How School Remakes Mind and Society.* Cambridge: Cambridge University Press.

Säljö, R. (2010). Digital Tools and Challenges to Institutional Traditions of Learning: Technologies, Social Memory and the Performative Nature of Learning. *Journal of Computer Assisted Learning, 26*(1), 53–64.

Weick, C. (1976). Educational Organizations as Loosely Coupled Systems. *Administrative Science Quarterly, 21*, 1–9.

Yin, R. (2010). Analytic Generalization. *Encyclopedia of Case Study Research, 1*, 20–22.

5 Affordances of digital technologies in pedagogical practices
A review

Investigating affordances

As mentioned in Chapter 2, Gibson (1979) originally referred to trans-actions between animals and environments when he wrote about af-fordances, but when applied as an analytical concept, it often refers to possibilities and constraints of resources in the environment. In our context, the focus is on what digitalized learning contexts offer teachers and students as agents. In some cases, people develop digital practices that are in line with what the developers of the digital re-sources intended. However, other practices are not necessarily results of the intentions engineers or programmers built into the resources. Sometimes the affordances that emerge might surprise the developers. Hence, it is through *interaction* between humans and digital technolo-gies as artifacts that the affordances emerge.

Research on affordances can sensitize teachers towards 'respons-ability' when faced with digital choices. Sterling (2014) introduced 'respons-ability' as a term in the discussion about sus-tainability. People need to learn how to live sustainably, he claims, which demands that we become able to respond to the opportuni-ties and challenges that persist beyond the current situation. This is also the case when it comes to digitalization. HE institutions, teachers, and students need to develop the ability to respond to challenges and opportunities triggered by continuous develop-ment of, access to, and use of digital technologies. Research-based knowledge will strengthen the respons-ability of educators. In this chapter, we therefore look into the pedagogical and didactical affordances of digital technologies in higher education and with teacher education as an epistemic lens.

Review and findings

We present the results of a search inspired by guidelines for scoping reviews and overview reviews. Scoping reviews involve doing "secondary research" (Major, Warwick, Rasmussen, Ludvigsen & Cook, 2018) through searching, collecting, evaluating, and presenting evidence found from analyzing results across a broad range of published studies (Arksey & O'Malley, 2005). Cluster results and evidence gaps can be identified, and the methodology is used to identify "key features of a diverse body of research in a connected manner" (Major et al., 2018, p. 1996). Several researchers (e.g., O'Flaherty & Phillips, 2015) highlight that this is particularly relevant in domains breaking new ground. In our case, the new ground we investigate is educational affordances of digital technologies.

In line with the guidelines given by Boote and Beile (2005), we have mainly mapped texts through searches in databases, but also by consulting experts. Oria (https://www.bibsys.no/oria-ny-soketjeneste-for-studenter-og-forskere/), "a portal to all the material that is available in Norwegian academic and research libraries, including a great extent of electronic material from open sources", was used to facilitate searches. Oria includes access to approximately 1,000 weekly updated resources, e.g., journals from Taylor & Francis, Routledge, Emerald, and Sage.

To provide an overall picture of research that gives insight into affordances of digital technologies in an HE context, we searched for texts with the term "review" in the title. In addition, all articles should include the following terms (at least once) in the texts: "higher education" AND "digital technologies" AND "quality" AND "teacher education". Even though "quality" is a complex and fuzzy cluster concept, it is also used as an everyday concept and left us with more relevant hits than "affordance". "Affordance" is a subject-specific term, typically used by a more selective group with a specific culture-sociological profile. Based on trying different search strategies, we found that texts discussing digital technologies in combination with "quality" issues often resulted in a demonstration of affordances, including critical aspects. Also, the term "teacher education" was included. Teacher education must have other technology-rich contexts in mind as they are responsible for preparing their students to work as teachers in schools where students usually have rich access to digital technologies and with an eye to new professional practices and even professional fields (designers of virtual worlds, developers of algorithms) emerging. Including articles from teacher education further helps us prepare the ground for the cases presented in Chapter 7. Other criteria were applied (in line with Creswell, 2012):

1 Peer-reviewed full-text articles
2 Published between 2014 and 2019
3 Written in English

Six hundred and five articles were listed. First, we screened titles and keywords to find that the relevance of the articles with our algorithm in mind dropped dramatically when approaching 100. Therefore, titles, keywords, and abstracts of the first 100 articles were reread in detail. We realized that the search included many diverse reviews (systematic/thematic/critical/historical), but also articles about single studies published in journals with "review" in the journal title. We excluded the studies that were not relevant for HE, like studies about digitalization in noneducational contexts and studies about HE but about other issues than educational affordances (e.g., transnational collaboration among researchers, e-leadership, the changing role of librarians in a digital age) This left us with 28 articles that clearly focused on digitalization, were relevant for HE, and gave insight into educational affordances – including educational challenges that seem to emerge in digital environments. Many articles focused on HE and a few on digitalization in K–12 and HE. One review that only investigated digitalization in K–12 was included, because it clearly identified some affordances that, from our point of view, seemed relevant across educational contexts and levels.

We listed the 28 titles with abstracts and took short notes about the thematic focus, main findings, and type of study (type of review/single study) presented in the texts. A very brief synthesis of this is presented in Table 5.1 to give a snapshot of the educational practices that were documented between 2014 and 2019.

Table 5.1 Overview of the studies included in the review

Themes addressed	Single studies	Reviews	Total number
21st-century skills (digital communication/ collaboration/interaction/computational thinking)	3	6	9
Educational models (blended learning/mobile learning/flipped classroom/online HE/MOOCs)	4	8	10
Digital learning resources (videos/podcasts/ OERs/apps/games/audio feedback)	2	5	5

In the following, we present the results of the review by synthetizing what the included reviews and empirical studies reveal about affordances. First, we put the spotlight on the emergence of new educational models, second on developing 21st-century skills through digital practices, and third on the use of specific digital learning resources in knowledge work.

Educational models

We start out with the most frequent theme of the included articles: educational models. In Figure 5.1, we illustrate how educational models that emerge in digital environments typically differ.

The illustration is a simplified representation and overlaps between models frequently occur in the reviewed literature. Six of the ten articles about educational models are about the use of digital technology on campus or in classrooms. Three are reviews (Baran, 2014; Pedro, Barbosa, & Santos, 2018; Pimmer, Mateescu, & Gröhbiel, 2016) and one is a single study about mobile learning (m-learning) (Royle, Stager, & Traxler, 2014). M-learning refers to learning that takes place

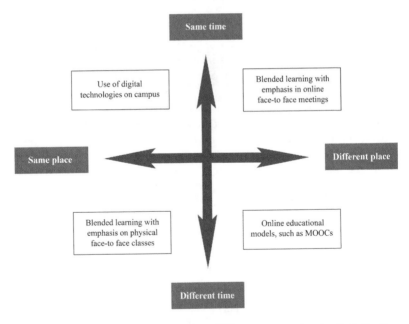

Figure 5.1 Four main models showing different approaches to digitalization in HE.

Source: Translated and with permission from Fossland, 2015, p. 33.

across contexts "through social and content interactions, using personal electronic devices" (Crompton, 2013, p. 4). Typical personal electronic devices are PCs, iPads, mobile phones, etc. that are used to collaborate and network across time and space.

Baran (2014) finds that m-learning in education seems to increase student engagement, extend their learning experiences, and stimulate the development of new literacies. Further, mobile technologies invite students to investigate things scientifically, engage in rich language learning contexts, explore the "real world", and organize mobile learning spaces. Due to this research, an affordance of mobile technologies is enhanced collaboration; mentoring and professional learning can strengthen relationships between teachers and students, personalize learning experiences, give learners timely access to resources, invite them to engage in knowledge production and share but also reflect upon, and discuss educational experiences. M-learning also invites frequent learning activities that link formal education with informal and personalized learning (Pimmer et al., 2016). Thus, unpacking m-learning demonstrates the presence of epistemic dimensions that are rare or not found in reproductive and mono-directional educational models. But Royle et al. (2014) find that there is also a tension between an educational wish to standardize practices, on the one hand, and efforts to promote context-specific and user-defined knowledge creation, on the other. People's use and access to mobile technologies raise challenges and questions concerning the validity of existing educational systems. Similarly, Pedro et al. (2018) suggest promoting educational validity through flexible m-learning. We consider this type of validity as ecological validity, i.e., that any experiment, intervention, and analysis must be consistent with the participants' definition of situations as these occur in everyday settings (Barowy & Jouper, 2004).

Research clearly indicates that mobile technologies have some positive affordances, in particular when it comes to engaging students in active and context-sensitive collaborative learning. However, the evidence for institutional legitimization in HE is still limited (Pimmer et al., 2016). Also, theoretical frameworks are often absent. The fact that m-learning is primarily reported as beneficial (Baran, 2014) might also be worth questioning. For instance, use of mobile technology can disturb group dynamics, and constant access to mobile technologies might be 'addictive' (Pedro et al., 2018) in the sense that their social and entertainment affordances detract from epistemic work. For instance, efforts to multitask might be an affordance that interferes with students' learning processes. Kirschner and De Bruyckere (2017) recently claimed that "the ability to multitask, does not exist" and that "designing education that assumes the presence of this ability hinders rather than helps learning" (p. 135). In addition, m-learning generates some ethical challenges regarding cyberbullying, issues of privacy, and unwanted exposure. In an effort to enhance educational quality and validity by taking better advantage of mobile technology in HE, such risks must be taken into account.

Also, the two reviews about flipped classroom (Lundin, Bergviken Rensfeldt, Hillman, Lantz-Andersson, & Peterson, 2018; O'Flaherty & Phillips, 2015) are related to how digital technologies can be used on campus. 'Flipping the classroom' implies that students are introduced to resources, often video lectures that they work with before class. In class, students typically take an active role in, e.g., group-based problem-solving where they use knowledge from having worked with the resources made available. There are indications that flipped learning helps teachers to renew the curriculum, give students a more active role, and promote the development of lifelong learners, and "The flipped model has the potential to enable teachers to cultivate critical and independent thought in their students, building the capacity for life-long learning" (O'Flatherty & Phillips, 2015, p. 94). The research interest in flipped learning is growing fast and the educational model is particularly popular in STEM subjects (science, technology, engineering, and math) (Lundin et al., 2018). However, studies about flipped learning also often lack clear models and theoretical frameworks. Also, data are often of local and anecdotal character resulting in sometimes questionable evidence of improved academic performance and student and staff satisfaction with the flipped approach (Lundin et al., 2018; O'Flatherty & Phillips, 2015). Consequently, it is difficult to make generalizable knowledge claims and "identify when, under what circumstances and in what ways the flipped classroom approach might be relevant as a pedagogical choice" (Lundin et al., 2018, p. 17).

Three single studies (Chen, 2014; Gil-Jaurena & Domínguez, 2018; Norberg, 2017) and three reviews (Brown, 2016; Buhl, 2018; Lee, 2017) focused on blended learning initiatives, massive open online courses (MOOCs), and online higher education. Blended learning models are usually developed to make studies more accessible to students, an often-mentioned affordance of digital technologies. Brown (2016) reviewed literature about faculty members' adoption and use of online tools for face-to-face instruction in blended instructional practice and identified six issues that influence how online tools were incorporated: faculty members' interactions with technology, academic workload, institutional context, interactions with students, the instructors' attitudes and beliefs about teaching, and opportunities for professional development. Brown (2016) demonstrated that teachers' exploration and use of affordances that digital technology offers in blended learning practices depends on technical, social, cultural, institutional, relational, and personal factors. In a pilot case study, Nordberg (2017) tried to solve a problem that seems to be relevant to blended learning designs, but also to MOOCs—that students easily procrastinate knowledge work within such models. By introducing time shift mechanisms between synchronous and asynchronous modes and facilitating interactive work processes similar to those in working life, the students developed better workflow and became more satisfied with their educational presence and progression. Nordberg's (2017) study addresses a common challenge in HE—that students are left too much to themselves and might drop out (Buhl, 2018; Chen, 2014; Gil-Jaurena & Domínguez, 2018). However, the study shows that this could be solved through a teacher's educational or didactic measures, like those mentioned above. In Chapter 8, we will follow up on this, as we present teachers as designers.

MOOC is the most flexible educational model and is typically developed to give people and societies access to education, independent of time and space. The "massiveness" and "openness" in MOOCs fuel an evolution towards more adapted learning, collaborative learning, and assessment supported by technical tools (Gil-Jaurena & Domínguez, 2018). Chen (2014) also finds that MOOCs benefit the learners, providers, and faculty who develop and teach them. However, the course quality, high dropout rates, unavailable course credits, ineffective assessment systems, complex copyright issues, and limited hardware are questioned. MOOCs seem to cause fragmented educational responsibility and weaker alignment between planning, teaching, and assessment. Also, a key challenge is complexity (Buhl, 2018; Gil-Jaurena & Dominquez, 2018) – issues related to scaling up into the thousands and students' intellectual development and critical thinking in such an environment may prove to be too much to the students. Teachers therefore need to invest in structuring and scaffolding their students' knowledge work. The research indicates that learning activities in MOOCs should be better adapted to the specific contexts, students should be more involved in developing the courses, and in general they need to be better stimulated as self-directed learners.

Lee (2017) questions the tendency to treat distance education as a single domain, while it actually takes several very different forms: asynchronous or synchronous, massively open or small and private, part of a blended program or as a stand-alone environment, etc. (Kaplan & Haenlein, 2016). Nevertheless, HE typically celebrates growth in online higher education as an innovative way to increase people's access to university education.

This review shows that an initial affordance of digitalization is redesigned programs and courses in HE; digitalization affords a re-configuration of programs but for diverse reasons and with different approaches depending on local context and educational purpose.

21st-century skills – and beyond

Researchers and policymakers continuously try to identify the most relevant skills for our time, often labeled 21st-century skills. The European Commission's science and knowledge service (2016) has, for instance, developed a Skills Agenda for Europe. They present critical thinking, entrepreneurship, problem–solving, and digital competences as skills that will allow people to develop good-quality jobs and fulfill their potential as confident, active citizens. Based on the Future of Jobs Survey, the World Economic Forum recently identified that some of the top relevant skills seem to change (Centre for the New Economy and Society, 2018). While "Analytical thinking and innovation" was the first of the top ten skills in 2018 and is also listed as the top trending skill of 2022, the survey indicated that "active learning and learning strategies" and "creativity, originality and initiative" will become more and more valued. Interestingly, "Attention to detail and trustworthiness" does not appear on the list over trending skills in 2022. Even if trending skills change,

> much of what distinguishes 21st century skills from 20th century competencies is that a person and a tool, application, medium or environment work in concert to accomplish an objective that is otherwise unobtainable (such as remote collaboration of a team scattered across the globe via groupware).
>
> (Dede, 2010, p. 64)

Three single studies focused on how digital technologies were used to enhance students' communication, collaboration, social interaction, and development of computational thinking (Hew & Cheung, 2013; Mohamedhoesein, 2017; Percell, 2016). The same applies to six reviews (Buitrago Flórez et al., 2017; Lantz-Andersson, Lundin, & Selwyn, 2018; Macaulay, Betts, Stiller, & Kellezi, 2018; Major et al., 2018; Tess, 2013; Yadav, Tiruwa, & Suri, 2017). Much of the referenced literature demonstrates that teachers and students use digital technologies to enhance collaboration, communication, and interaction, which is considered to have a positive impact on student learning. For instance, Hew and Chieng (2013) suggest that dialogic, constructionist, or co-constructive pedagogy supported by activities such as Socratic questioning, peer review, and self-reflection seems to increase student achievement in blog, wiki, and 3D immersive virtual world environments. Collaboration in wikis further generates big data that can be used to inform instructional practices (Percell, 2016). Internet-based learning (IBL) platforms afford collaborative learning that might transform the traditional class and teacher-centric educational system, making teaching and learning more interactive and informative (Yadav, Tiruwa, & Suri, 2017). Major et al. (2018) emphasize that some teachers make use of digital environments to expose students to a variety of perspectives, promote challenging dialogues, and engage them in the co-construction of knowledge. In addition, students can externalize and share ideas and competence through multiple modes in digital contexts and through digital resources. Through such processes, autonomy, inclusive learning communities, and motivation to engage in collective learning processes can be promoted. Further, students' use of digital technologies and digitally distributed interaction enhance their sense of belonging, trigger engagement in discussions, and promote study persistence of minority students (Mohamedhoesein, 2017).

These competencies resonate with the much promoted 21st-century skills such as complex problem-solving, creativity, and collaboration. Taken together, the above studies can also be read as nutshelling the skills and competencies needed to meet the shift in epistemology and epistemic work we have outlined in previous chapters. But the affordances identified in the reviewed literature also demonstrate that they depend on teachers' and/or students' agency. There are also indications that lack of technical skills, a weak knowledge base, digitalization disengaged from learning, and digital distraction inhibit technology supported, dialogic teaching and learning. However, we argue that our review points to a variety of educational transformations that on an aggregated level make an impact on HE, as well as on epistemic work as well as how we organize it.

Today, students and teachers are also increasingly expected to learn programming and develop computational thinking (Buitrago Flórez et al., 2017). Buitrago Flórez et al. (2017) argue that students through programming will develop computational skills, but also thinking skills, as they use concepts from computing and information science to solve problems and experience designing and evaluating complex information systems and, thus, also learn to understand human reasoning and behavior. Thus, we see a skills perspective that is much broader and comprehensive than for merely instrumental programming or 'coding' purposes.

An affordance that is presented as a two-edged sword in the literature is digital networking. Lantz-Andersson et al. (2018) observe a growing tendency that teachers establish and use informal, digital networks to develop as professionals. Both formal and informal digital teacher networks seem to support and promote collective development of professional practices. Participants typically experience that the networks engage them emotionally and trigger reflection even if the professional 'climate' is characterized by consensus and conformity (Lantz-Andersson et al., 2018). But there are also examples of networks where people offend each other and where cyberbullying is a growing problem (Macaulay et al., 2018). The possibility to remain anonymous in digital networks might explain why.

To what extent and how should HE in general respond to such social challenges? If we agree that HE institutions should qualify students for working life, but also offer an arena for socialization and personal growth (Biesta, 2009), it is obvious that HE needs to take action as such challenges emerge. As Washington (2014) has shown, cyberbullying in HE (and in the workplace) is a direct result of cyberbullying in previous schooling but accelerates with mobile technologies. When it comes to digital bullying, Macaulay et al. (2018) suggest that students should learn more about safe internet use. From our perspective, HE is also in position to foster respectful behavior and develop decency of expression. Professors, faculty, staff, and fellow students may all be expected to monitor online behavior. This is a delicate issue where privacy meets surveillance and should be approached accordingly. Digital bullying is just one of the ethical challenges that arise in digital societies and illustrates that digitalization generates questions concerning not only how we educate but also how students should socialize online through their studies. The emergence of social media firestorms or digital intolerance and hate groups could be added to the list of really serious digital challenges that call for an informed HE response.

To summarize this section, the reviewed articles suggest that digital technologies can be used to prepare students for the 21st century by providing them with digital skills, competencies, and experiences as collaborative, communicating, networking, caring learners. However, the studies demonstrate that these affordances do not emerge automatically, but depend on the agency of teachers and students who design learning situations and actively engage in them. Also, experiences that might disturb students and their learning can appear. This is why we argue that digital technologies must be recognized as artifacts that potentially stimulate meaningful epistemic work (and, thus, enhance HE quality), but also potentially cause epistemological and social challenges.

Digital learning resources

Having moved from educational models through a series of skills and competencies, the review also identified a more specific focus on digital resources. Three single studies (Blomgren, 2018; Kelly, 2014; Laaser & Toloza, 2017) and four reviews (Dixon, 2015; Gaudin & Chaliès, 2015; Stevenson & Hedberg, 2017; Vlachopoulos & Makri, 2017) focus on the affordances found in, e.g., open educational resources (OERs), videos, apps, audio feedback, and games. Even if they differ in character, they all have in common that such digital resources come with intentions for students to enhance their learning. That is why we categorize them as digital learning resources.

OERs are either from public domains or made free through licenses. Many are designed for education, while others are repurposed by educators. OERs promote cost-saving and provide access to user-generated content. Use of OERs can potentially stimulate instructor creativity and timely learning opportunities aligned with the interests and needs of learners (Blomgren, 2018). However, ease of use is vital in the adoption of OERs, and creators of OERs need to keep both audience and usability in mind when they develop them (Kelly, 2014). Blomgren (2018) finds that there is a need to develop shared perceptions of the purposes and practical use of specific OERs and elevate the quality of educational resources. But as always, no matter how sophisticated the artifacts are, human activity is what determines its educational value.

What about, e.g., digital games or feedback from virtual entities? Can these qualify as potential learning resources? Vlachopoulos and Makri (2017) systematically reviewed research literature on games and simulation pedagogy in higher education and examined its impact on achievement of specific learning objectives. According to the authors, results indicate that games and/or simulations have a positive impact on cognitive, behavioral, and affective learning goals. For instance, gaming invites playfulness and problem-based learning and can promote content understanding and concept learning, but also self-assessment and higher order thinking skills. Further, simulations can let students observe the consequences of their actions and decision-making, which might lead to active, transformative, and experiential knowledge work. However, the learning outcome of gaming depends on how the teachers incorporate games and design their teaching, and most researchers conclude that games should be treated as supplementary elements in education. Dixon (2015) reviewed research about audio feedback and found that such feedback seemed to improve both students' learning and the teaching process because it is considered personal and therefore strengthens the relations between teaching staff and learners.

Videos have become quite common learning resources in HE and are often developed by teachers without further experience with media production. Thus, the required quality of videos used in online education seems to be lacking, according to Laaser and Toloza (2017). They find that possibilities in video productions are not sufficiently exploited in typical educational videos found on the web and claim that HE lacks adequate incentives for teachers to explore and take advantage of the potentials in video production. For instance, videos can be designed to enhance students' collaborative learning. Gadudin and Chaliès (2015) write a less critical article about videos. They focus on videos of teachers that are used as means to professionalize the teacher role. They find that teachers and student teachers who produce and watch videos of themselves while teaching or watch videos of other teachers in action are motivated and improve their classroom practices. Professional development, then, emerges as one identifiable affordance of digital video resources (Gaudin & Chaliès, 2015).

In sum, the literature on a selection of digital learning resources demonstrates that they are ripe with diverse affordances – from being free and flexible to being used for professional development. Also, providing students and teachers with access to enormous amounts of rapidly changing digital resources is democratic in the sense that it challenges a tradition where few people have had the power to define what is relevant for a group of students to read or relate to. Also, such resources, by being malleable and often collaboratively oriented, invite students and teachers to engage in deep learning processes required for complex problem-solving. However, when it comes to comparing and selecting resources, Stevenson and Hedberg (2017) suggest that teachers should design challenging learning tasks independently of the technology and rather invite students to move beyond limitations found in the individual app and use multiple apps ('app smashing') when they solve the tasks. This will move students beyond the underlying limitations of individual apps, and they will develop a wide range of digital skills as they decide which apps to use, the authors argue. The emphasis on task design is interesting in light of our focus on teaching as a design science and teachers as designers (see Chapters 6 and 8).

Affordances challenging inertia

In the first few chapters of this book, we introduced theoretical concepts and perspectives that we find have explanatory power when studying and discussing digitalization in HE. We argued that theoretical anchoring is often lacking and the present review supports the claim. We have found that many studies are not located in a conceptual or epistemological landscape. Several of the articles also have a "pro-digital-practices-tone" that probably could be better balanced by also including attention to risks. Stronger theoretical anchoring could, as Lundin et al. (2018) suggest, help researchers examine educational practices that emerge in digital environments more fully and critically, instead of too often base assumptions about knowledge on anecdotal 'evidence'.

Nevertheless, our review shows that digitalization – despite documented or anecdotal evidence of HE inertia and traditionalism – impacts learning and teaching practices and, therefore, has epistemological and social implications. It indicates that digital technologies invite universities to develop new educational models and practices. In particular, the review indicates that access to digital technologies invites universities to explore m-learning, 'flipped' educational practices, develop MOOCs, blended learning designs, create dialogic spaces where students exchange perspectives and co-construct knowledge, etc. Constraints in time and space are gradually suspended, and access to information is infinite.

The crux is to use these affordances for epistemic work of high quality, beneficial to students as well as the larger society. No practices are developed without teachers' and students' mutual and collaborative agency. Hence, humans and digital technologies are intertwined, and when knowledge production and epistemic practices are transformed as a result of such intertwining, changes in the knowers follow. The epistemic principle of "we-know-the world as we change it" is connected to the ontological principle of "we-come-to-be-as-we-change-the-world" (Stetsenko, 2017, p. 197). Mostly, the articles we have reviewed focus on affordances of computers and the development of quite well-known digital practices or resources (e.g., new educational models, videos, and audio feedback). Consequently, the review only hints at how affordances of digital technologies will challenge inertia in HE. The advent of robotics, artificial intelligence, virtual reality, and bio-engineering invoke notions of *'Frankenscience'* and man–machine hybridity (Nagy, Wylie, Eschrich, & Finn, 2019). Such issues will briefly be revisited in Chapter 8. But first, in Chapter 6, we present and discuss efforts to identify what competencies HE teachers need in order to utilize affordances and prevent the education-related risk factors associated with digitalization.

References

Arksey, H., & O'Malley, L. (2005). Scoping Studies: Towards a Methodological Framework. *International Journal of Social Research Methodology, 8*(1), 19–32.

Baran, E. (2014). A Review of Research on Mobile Learning in Teacher Education. *Educational Technology & Society, 17*(4), 17–32.

Barowy, W., & Jouper, C. (2004). The Complex of School Change: Personal and Systemic Codevelopment. *Mind, Culture and Activity, 11*(1), 9–24.

Biesta, G. (2009). Good Education in an Age of Measurement: On the Need to Reconnect with the Question of Purpose in Education. *Educational Assessment, Evaluation and Accountability, 21*(1), 33–46.

Blomgren, C. (2018). OER Awareness and Use: The Affinity between Higher Education and K-12. *International Review of Research in Open and Distance Learning, 19*(2). doi:10.19173/irrodl.v19i2.3431

Brown, M. G. (2016). Blended Instructional Practice: A Review of the Empirical Literature on Instructors' Adoption and Use of Online Tools in Face-to-face Teaching. *The Internet and Higher Education, 31*, 1–10. doi:10.1016/j.iheduc.2016.05.001

Buhl, M. (2018). Upscaling the Number of Learners, Fragmenting the Role of Teachers: How do Massive Open Online Courses (MOOCs) Form New Conditions for Learning Design? *International Review of Education, 64*(2), 179–195. doi:10.1007/s11159-018-9714-1

Buitrago Flórez, F., Casallas, R., Hernández, M., Reyes, A., Restrepo, S., & Danies, G. (2017). Changing a Generation's Way of Thinking: Teaching Computational Thinking through Programming. *Review of Educational Research, 87*(4), 834–860. doi:10.3102/0034654317710096

Chen, Y. (2014). Investigating MOOCs through Blog Mining. *International Review of Research in Open and Distance Learning, 15*(2), 85–106.

Crompton, H. (2013). A Historical Overview of Mobile Learning: Toward Learner-Centered Education. In Z. L. Berge & L. Y. Muilenburg (Eds.), *Handbook of Mobile Learning*. New York, NY: Routledge (pp. 3–14).

Dede, C. (2010). Comparing Frameworks for 21st Century Skills. In J. Bellanca & R. Brandt (Eds.), *21st Century Skills: Rethinking How Students Learn* (pp. 51–75). Bloomington, IN: Solution Tree Press.

Dixon, S. (2015). The Pastoral Potential of Audio Feedback: A Review of the Literature. *Pastoral Care in Education. 33*(2), 96–104.

Fossland, T. (2015). *Digitale læringsformer i høyere utdanning*. Oslo: Universitetsforlaget.

Gaudin, C., & Chaliès, S. (2015). Video Viewing in Teacher Education and Professional Development: A Literature Review. *Educational Research Review, 16*, 41–67.

Gil-Jaurena, I., & Domínguez, D. (2018). Teachers' Roles in Light of Massive Open Online Courses (MOOCs): Evolution and Challenges in Higher Distance Education. *International Review of Education, 64*(2), 197–219. doi:10.1007/s11159-018-9715-0

Hew, K. F., & Cheung, W. S. (2013). Use of Web 2.0 Technologies in K-12 and Higher Education: The Search for Evidence-based Practice. *Educational Research Review, 9*(1), 47–64. doi:10.1016/j.edurev.2012.08.001

Kaplan, A. M., & Haenlein, M. (2016). Higher Education and the Digital Revolution: About MOOCs, SPOCs, Social Media, and the Cookie Monster. *Business Horizons, 59*, 441–450.

Kelly, H. (2014). A Path Analysis of Educator Perceptions of Open Educational Resources Using the Technology Acceptance Model. *International Review of Research in Open and Distance Learning, 15*(2), 26–42. doi:10.19173/irrodl.v15i2.1715

Kirschner, P. A., & De Bruyckere, P. (2017). The Myths of the Digital Native and the Multitasker. *Teaching and Teacher Education, 67*, 135–142.

Laaser, W., & Toloza, E. (2017). The Changing Role of the Educational Video in Higher Distance Education. *International Review of Research in Open and Distance Learning, 18*(2). doi:10.19173/irrodl.v18i2.3067

Lantz-Andersson, A., Lundin, M., & Selwyn, N. (2018). Twenty Years of Online Teacher Communities: A Systematic Review of Formally-Organized and Informally-Developed Professional Learning Groups. *Teaching and Teacher Education, 75*, 302–315. doi:10.1016/j.tate.2018.07.008

Lee, K. (2017). Rethinking the Accessibility of Online Higher Education: A Historical Review. *The Internet and Higher Education, 33*, 15–23. doi:10.1016/j.iheduc.2017.01.001

Lundin, M., Bergviken Rensfeldt, A., Hillman, T., Lantz-Andersson, A., & Peterson, L. (2018). Higher Education Dominance and Siloed Knowledge: A Systematic Review of Flipped Classroom Research. *International Journal of Educational Technology in Higher Education, 15*(1), 1–30. doi:10.1186/s41239-018-0101-6

Macaulay, P. J. R., Betts, L. R., Stiller, J., & Kellezi, B. (2018). Perceptions and Responses Towards Cyberbullying: A Systematic Review of Teachers in the Education System. *Aggression and Violent Behavior, 43*, 1–12. doi:10.1016/j.avb.2018.08.004

Major, L., Warwick, P., Rasmussen, I., Ludvigsen, S., & Cook, V. (2018). Classroom Dialogue and Digital Technologies: A Scoping Review. *The Official Journal of the IFIP Technical Committee on Education, 23*(5), 1995–2028. doi:10.1007/s10639-018-9701-y

Mohamedhoesein, N. (2017). The Use of ICT by Second-Year College Students and Its Relation with Their Interaction and Sense of Belonging. *Open Review of Educational Research, 4*(1), 177–191.

Nagy, P., Wylie, R., Eschrich, J., & Finn, E. (2019). Facing the Pariah of Science: The Frankenstein Myth as a Social and Ethical Reference for Scientists. *Science and Engineering Ethics*. doi:10.1007/s11948-019-00121-3

Norberg, A., Stöckel, B., & Antti, M. L. (2017). Time Shifting and Agile Time Boxes in Course Design. *The International Review of Research in Open and Distributed Learning, 18*(6). doi:10.19173/irrodl.v18i6.3182

O'Flaherty, J., & Phillips, C. (2015). The Use of Flipped Classrooms in Higher Education: A Scoping Review. *The Internet and Higher Education, 25*, 85–95.

Pedro, L., Barbosa, C., & Santos, C. (2018). A Critical Review of Mobile Learning Integration in Formal Educational Contexts. *International Journal of Educational Technology in Higher Education, 15*(1), 1–15. doi:10.1186/s41239-018-0091-4

Percell, J. C. (2016). Data Collaborative: A Practical Exploration of Big Data in Course Wikis (Report). *Quarterly Review of Distance Education, 17*(4), 63.

Pimmer, C., Mateescu, M., & Gröhbiel, U. (2016). Mobile and Ubiquitous Learning in Higher Education Settings. A Systematic Review of Empirical Studies. *Computers in Human Behavior, 63*, 490–501. doi:10.1016/j.chb.2016.05.057

Royle, K., Stager, S., & Traxler, J. (2014). Teacher Development with Mobiles: Comparative Critical Factors. *Quarterly Review of Comparative Education, 44*(1), 29–42. doi:10.1007/s11125-013-9292-8

Sterling, S. (2014). 'At Variance with Reality': How to Re-think Our Thinking'. *The Journal of Sustainability Education* (Vol. 6, May 2914). Retrieved July 15, 2019, from jsedimensions.org/wordpress/wp-content/uploads/2014/05/Sterling-Stephen-JSE-May-2014-PDF-Ready.pdf

Stevenson, M. E., & Hedberg, J. G. (2017). Mobilizing Learning: A Thematic Review of Apps in K-12 and Higher Education. *Interactive Technology and Smart Education, 14*(2), 126–137. doi:10.1108/ITSE-02-2017-0017

Tess, P. A. (2013). The Role of Social Media in Higher Education Classes (Real and Virtual) – A Literature Review. *Computers in Human Behavior, 29*(5), A60–A68. doi:10.1016/j.chb.2012.12.032

Vlachopoulos, D., & Makri, A. (2017). The Effect of Games and Simulations on Higher Education: A Systematic Literature Review. *International Journal of Educational Technology in Higher Education, 14*, 1–33. doi:10.1186/S41239-017-0062-1

Washington, E. T. (2014). An Overview of Cyberbullying in Higher Education. *Adult Learning, 26*(1), 21–27.

Yadav, R., Tiruwa, A., & Suri, P. K. (2017). Internet Based Learning (IBL) in Higher Education: A Literature Review. *Journal of International Education in Business, 10*(2), 102–129. doi:10.1108/JIEB-10-2016-0035

6 A response to digitalization
Professional digital competence

Throughout the previous chapters, we have outlined a number of issues, questions, and challenges that arise in the wake of digitalization. Partly, they have been connected to epistemology (and ontology), partly to educational quality, partly to educational leadership and institutional strategies and partly to affordances of digital technologies. A key message is that digitalization contributes to transform human agents and vice versa (for seminal studies, see, e.g., Castells, 1996, 1997, 1998; Cope & Kalantzis, 2000; Gee, Hull, & Lankshear, 1996; Stetsenko, 2017). Thus, in our HE context, an essential question that surfaces is what kind of *competence(s)* students and teachers need in order to engage with digital resources to foster knowledge advancement and prepare students for society and working life. Our review in Chapter 5 gave us some indication as to what models, skills, and resources to master. However, a more comprehensive competence framework did not emerge. This is the theme of this chapter.

Competence, mastery, and appropriation

But before we move into the issue of competence, one conceptual maneuver is necessary; we must clarify the distinction between mastery and appropriation. At the heart of any competence is a blend of skills and deep understanding of what is required in order to perform a task, execute an operation, or make sense of a phenomenon that rises above the mundane and repetitive everyday chores. There are many definitions of competence, often linked to a particular and personal ability, quality, or state. However, we firmly connect competence to practices and contexts, developed and enacted in a collective zone of proximal development with more knowledgeable peers and available cultural resources (Engeström, 1987; Vygotsky, 1978).

Developing such competence requires personal investment beyond acquiring a certain mastery over situations and practices. To instrumentally master a plethora of digital resources is one thing, a deep understanding of them and how they may transform situations and one's own opportunities, professional enactment, and lifeworld requires more than even sophisticated mastery; it requires *appropriation*. Appropriation differs from mastery in the sense that mastery can be exercised as control over tools; it is basically instrumental, unidirectional, and manipulative. Appropriation, on the other hand, involves transformation of tools and contexts as well as agents but not necessarily without resistance. In the following, appropriation is used for its explanatory power when we study how students and academics face digitalization. It is inseparable from what we have chosen to name *professional digital competence* (PDC).

Appropriation involves taking 'something' that belongs to others and giving it a meaningful dimension in one's own life. Bakhtin (1979/2000), in his oft-cited passage on language, offers an eloquent explanation:

> As a living, socio-ideological concrete thing, as heteroglot opinion, language, for the individual consciousness, lies on the borderline between oneself and the other. The word in language is half someone else's. It becomes "one's own" only when the speaker populates it with his intention, with his own accent, when he appropriates the word, adapting it to his own semantic and expressive intention. Prior to this moment of appropriation the word does not exist in a neutral and impersonal language (it is not, after all, out of a dictionary that the speaker gets his words!), but rather it exists in other people's mouths, in other people's contexts, serving other people's intentions: it is from there that one must take the word, and make it one's own. (...) Language is not a neutral medium that passes freely and easily into the private property of the speaker's intentions; it is populated – overpopulated – with the intentions of others. Expropriating it, forcing it to submit to one's own intentions and accents, is a difficult and complicated process.
>
> (pp. 293–294)

Try substituting 'language' with 'digitalization' and 'word' with 'application' or 'digital resource', and we have Bakhtin nailing what developing digital competence involves and the related costs. Most digital resources were never developed for educational purposes, which means that educators must force them to "submit to one's own intentions".

Everybody who has only tangentially been involved in such efforts recognizes the challenges and risks; traditional learning environments and epistemologies were never developed with digitalization in mind. Consequently, we have to engage in the processes of *appropriation* in order to bring about *transformation*.

Our conclusion after this somewhat detailed excursion into conceptual underpinnings is that a competence framework for transformative, educational digitalization must center on humans trying to expand educational practices by making them "their own". This is not mastery; it is appropriation.

The many faces of 'digital competence'

Over the years, a series of models, descriptors, and descriptions have been developed to capture the required competence for educators in digital learning environments. A plethora of terms such as digital competence, digital literacy/literacies, information and communication technology (ICT) literacy, computer skills, digital skills, and internet skills have been used to describe the competencies teachers need to be professional in a digital age. Ilomäki, Paavola, Lakkala, and Kantosalo (2016) analyzed 76 articles that described digital competence using different terms and found the most common ones to be digital literacy, new literacies, multiliteracies, and media literacy. Often, the competences reflected a student perspective. However, Lankshear, Snyder, and Green (2000) took a comprehensive and principled approach to what digital literacy means for teachers. They labeled the juxtaposition of technology and literacy 'technoliteracy' – practices that have operational, cultural, and critical dimensions to be appropriated by teachers. They also connected school and out-of-school practices, a research topic that in recent years has raised a lot of interest (Ludvigsen, Lund, Rasmussen, & Säljö, 2010; Lund, 2016).

At the end of this chapter, we introduce the notion of PDC. PDC demands that teachers be able to connect the affordances of digital technologies to vital issues in the learning sciences, the discussion of appropriation (above) being one of them. The conceptually somewhat messy tradition has informed our development of four PDC principles. However, before we elaborate the concept and argue for its relevance, qualities, and significance, we first turn to three established models or frameworks and discuss their qualities and shortcomings, seen from the perspectives in this volume. Invoking all such frameworks would amount to a separate book, so we choose three influential frameworks as a backdrop: the Technological Pedagogical

Content Knowledge (TPACK) framework (Koehler & Mishra, 2009; Mishra & Koehler, 2006); the European Framework for the Digital Competence of Educators, DigCompEdu (Redecker, 2017); and the Substitution, Augmentation, Modification, and Redefinition (SAMR) model (Hamilton, Rosenberg, & Akcaoglu, 2016).

TPACK

The conceptual framework of TPACK (Koehler & Mishra, 2009; Mishra & Koehler, 2006) has been widely used to identify knowledge sources and domains teachers need to consider when integrating ICT into their teaching. TPACK builds on Shulman's (1986, 1987) notion of pedagogical content knowledge and has influenced efforts to integrate digitalization in education in a principled way. In the interplay between pedagogical knowledge, content knowledge, and technological knowledge, three additional components emerge: pedagogical content knowledge, technological content knowledge, and technological pedagogical knowledge. These merge in a TPACK core when combined.

By connecting digital competencies with pedagogical and subject-specific aspects, the TPACK model has exercised significant influence on educators. At its center, the model captures the hybrid competence and mutually constitutive dimensions of pedagogical and technological dimensions that often escape other models of digital competence. This has proved to be an obvious strength of the framework. But the model is less explicit when it comes to educational designs, educational practices, and issues of quality; how can we know or decide what kinds of practices to nurture and cultivate and why? This may be one reason why HE has not adopted the TPACK framework to the extent that pre-tertiary education has.

Additional reasons can be found in weaknesses emerging from literature reviews. One such review was conducted by Voogt, Fisser, Pareja Roblin, Tondeur, and van Braakt (2013) who reviewed 56 TPACK publications. They found little consensus on what TPACK entails; its components were difficult to distinguish; its core appeared as somewhat fuzzy, the concept of technology appeared indistinct, there were few instances of discipline-specific TPACK, and a student perspective was lacking. Similarly, Chai, Koh, and Tsai (2013) found in another review that the TPACK components created confusion due to possible overlap, which may result in teachers not going beyond existing practices or developing new ones, although TPACK may be intended to facilitate such efforts.

Lorentzen (2017) argued that the TPACK model is too harmonious and does not take into account transformation, tensions, breakdowns, disruptions, and contradictions that arise when educational practices become digitalized and unsettle historically established and 'proven' practices (Kaptelinin & Nardi, 2006; Lund, Furberg, Bakken, & Engelien, 2014; Lund & Rasmussen, 2008; Yamagata-Lynch, 2010). Thus, we see that problems with the TPACK framework may arise from the fact that it does not sufficiently address the transformative and epistemological issues that we in this volume seek to bring to the fore.

DigCompEdu

Also, a series of policy efforts have been made to identify digital competencies. Typically, these aim to develop national or transnational standards or frameworks that, although context sensitive, seek to establish a general reference frame to support the development of educator-specific digital competences. One of the recent and more elaborate references is the European Framework for the Digital Competence of Educators, DigCompEdu[1] (Redecker, 2017). The framework seeks to establish a common language and logic for digital competence. The result is a comprehensive document and with as many as 22 "elementary competences" organized in six areas.

Two dimensions are especially valuable to HE when applying this framework. First, the emphasis on professional engagement opens up for a perspective where digitalization transcends the more generic educational implications and connects it to diverse professions and, consequently, diverse knowledge domains. We will return to these issues when we discuss the PDC framework (below). Second, the DigCompEdu framework integrates learner and teacher perspectives, emphasizing the co-construction of knowledge work and mutual dependency of participants. The framework clearly adheres to a practice-oriented competence concept.

DigCompEdu aspires to be applicable in all types and levels of education while acknowledging existing, local efforts. But it also serves as a template for guiding educational policies for educationally relevant digitalization, and offers an instrument with which to map and 'measure' digital competence. This instrument focuses on three dimensions: competence areas, competence descriptors, and levels of mastery. These can serve as benchmarks that help educators assess their own progression as digitally competent. Thus, the notion of *stages* of competence development becomes crucial. The DigCompEdu framework operates with six stages: from Newcomer and Explorer to the highest stages of Pioneer. At the latter stage, educators are expected to critique existing practices and develop new ones. The framework is more than skills-oriented. For instance, it includes collaborative and self-regulated learning. However, it lacks focus on epistemic issues, digital artifacts, and how digitalization and transformation can be mutually constitutive of educational and professional development. Consequently, we argue that it does not sufficiently meet requirements and needs in the HE sector.

The SAMR model

The SAMR model, originally developed by Puentedura (2006), is constructed around four levels. The description of practices in each level of the 'ladder' indicates to what extent a teacher has developed relevant digital competence:

- *Substitution*: Existing tools and practices are merely replaced by digitalized versions without any functional change.
- *Augmentation*: Existing practices are sustained but also expanded due to digitalization, e.g., reading and writing as a multimodal competence.
- *Modification*: Digitalization affords redefinition and expansion of tasks and assignments, e.g., inquiry-based and student active learning using simulations instead of responding to textbook tasks.
- *Redefinition*: Digitalization allows for the creation of new tasks, previously inconceivable, e.g., engaging students in mass collaboration or producing podcasts.

The framework has gained popularity among practitioners, possibly because of its simplicity, but does not appear in scholarly literature to the extent of the frameworks we have briefly discussed above. The model is not (yet) theorized or connected to a conceptual framework that resonates with current issues in, e.g., the learning sciences. Still, we include it here because of its emphasis on tasks and assignments and its progression towards expansion, breaking away from a status quo, and going beyond current horizons – ambitious ambitions that clearly resonate with what the present volume promotes. The shift from enhancement to transformation appears clearly articulated.

But due to its lack of theoretical underpinnings, the SAMR model exposes itself to criticism. For instance, Hamilton, Rosenberg, and Akcaoglu (2016) in their critical review of the model claim that the model does not sufficiently acknowledge contextual factors: institutional, cultural, or educational. The result is overgeneralization and risk of being prescriptive. Thus, the complexity that emerges when learning, pedagogy, and instructional practices meet is not accounted for. Further, they argue that the structure is hierarchical and unidirectional with an ideal end point. But learning and instruction are characterized by cycles, reciprocity, serendipity, and context-sensitive designs. Consequently, the taxonomy risks are enacted as deterministic and linear, ignoring the dynamics and unexpected affordances in digitalized practices. Finally, they criticize that the product is prioritized over the process. The outcome is a particular instructional activity and not so much the learning processes involved.

Our conclusion is that there is nothing 'wrong' with the SAMR framework. It is easy to perceive it as 'intuitively right', hence its popularity with practitioners. But its attraction may fade if it is not linked to a conceptual framework with explanatory power that surpasses the 'one-size-fits-all' approach. It does not touch upon epistemologies, digital affordances, issues of educational quality, or goodness of fit with vastly different educational paradigms such as, e.g., behaviorism, cognitivism, or cultural–historical perspectives. In the following, we seek to invoke a framework that keeps the transformative dimensions from the SAMR model while including what we have found lacking.

Professional digital competence

We have briefly presented values and shortcomings of three major frameworks. They all attempt to identify what competencies teachers need in order to be professional in a digital context or how such competencies can be identified. One of the frameworks presented is research driven but seems difficult to operationalize, the other is policy driven with an emphasis on implementation of digital technologies and development of digital skills more than on epistemological design, and the third is practice-oriented and transformative but largely separated from research and conceptual frameworks. There are, of course, an abundance of additional and diverse frameworks,[2] but the three discussed above seem most relevant as a context and backdrop for the principles we promote with the PDC framework we now will present.

In the following, we will present four principles for what we call PDC in HE. However, a brief historical genesis is in place to show how we arrive at it. Initially, the Norwegian Centre for ICT in Education developed a framework for PDC designed for teachers in schools and teacher education (Kelentrić, Helland, & Arstorp, 2017). Several researchers were involved in operationalizing it, and in addition, it is based on a detailed review of relevant international frameworks for teachers' digital competence. As the initial component – *professional* – indicates, competence is linked to work-life processes, including epistemic work. Due to this framework, PDC for a teacher demands awareness of how subjects change in a digitalized society; competencies to relate school to such a changing society and initiate and engage in educational change processes; the ability to identify and address ethical questions and dilemmas that emerge in a digitalized society; the ability to design educational practices based on digital skills combined with pedagogical and didactic knowledge; and knowledge about how to lead learning processes and facilitate interaction and communication.

Even if the framework was developed for schools and teacher education, it can be applied in knowledge domains and HE programs beyond this, however, in adapted versions. For instance, the ethical issues relevant to address in a health program may vary from those to be addressed in an engineer program or in teacher education. Developing PDC in HE programs holds a dual undertaking. On the one hand, teachers need to have appropriated digitalization as an integrated element in their professional enactment. On the other hand, to support students in their knowledge work and prepare them for work life, teachers also need to foster students' PDC. Also students need to appropriate digitalization including its future-oriented and transformative epistemological dimensions. HE teachers must design for students to develop their own PDC so that they understand how digitalization represents opportunities to make *their* learning and knowledge production more relevant and goal oriented. This is a daunting endeavor but applies to all students and all studies from architecture to zoology. Thus, for teachers integrating PDC into HE, one vital challenge is to design learning environments and envisage learning trajectories conducive to their students' professional and epistemic development but also attend to the broader societal and ethical issues that loom on the horizon.

Due to this framework, PDC is complex. For instance, when identifying, developing, or using digital learning resources, a teacher with PDC will need to draw on pedagogical and didactic competencies, combined with subject-specific knowledge and digital skills. Digital learning resources provide a variety of opportunities for students and teachers to interact with disciplinary knowledge and subject-specific scientific discourses. In the natural sciences and in disciplines with high levels of abstraction (e.g., mathematics), simulations, modeling, programming, and augmented reality afford student manipulation of variables and, thus, engage them in research-like activities and, increasingly, haptic and tactile experiences. This has proved to increase students' conceptual understanding of complex processes (see, e.g., Lehtinen, 2010, scholarly literature is abundant). In language arts and language learning, ICT has boosted multimodal approaches; suspended constraints in communicative space and time; afforded polycontextuality; increasingly improved machine translation; given rise to collaborative annotation, new genres, and conventions; etc. In sum, we see representations in the form of new communication ecologies emerging (Hearn & Foth, 2007), which teachers within this field must relate to. In social sciences and history, digitalization has afforded immediate access to unlimited information. However, such information is often represented as fragmented, contested, and contradictory (just google any controversial issue) and requires students to synthesize and make meaning of the mosaic. Source criticism and sensitivity towards manipulation and 'fake news' become crucial. Also, digitalization has afforded representations (historical as well as for current affairs) through serious games (games developed for a purpose other than pure entertainment) and gamification (application of gamelike elements to educational activities) (Baptista & Oliveira, 2019).

The list of digitized, disciplinary representations could go on (aesthetic disciplines would require a separate volume with their plethora of novel representations in arts and crafts). Also, although the above listing seems compartmentalized, there are numerous overlaps and blended variants. The point is that relating to different digital representations of knowledge and knowing illustrates the more discipline-specific qualities of PDC (for an extended discussion of such discipline-specific representations, see Lund et al., 2014). The above examples should be enough to argue that digitalization implies subject-specific epistemologies, not merely general principles for how epistemic work can be carried out in digital learning environments. But the subject-specific issues hinted at here are only in their infancy when it comes to research and, thus, represent a major challenge for HE research and practice.

None of the PDC frameworks mentioned so far give preference to a specific paradigm or learning theoretical perspective. Opting for a theoretical perspective will, among other things, depend on the phenomenon under study, how and with what explanatory power to respond to research questions, educational problems, etc. We find that connecting PDC to cultural–historical activity theory (CHAT) (Engeström, 1987) offers explanatory and analytical power. The reason is that CHAT acknowledges that (digital) artifacts afford users to move beyond existing practices and pave the way for new ones. Epistemically, such efforts are not restricted to the individual mind but involve collaborative agency.

With the above backdrop and the discussion of what is at stake addressed in the previous chapters, we venture a set of four principles that to some extent are inspired by the presented frameworks. The principles are anchored in CHAT, are aligned to the HE context, and can be operationalized across programs and disciplines to promote productive engagement with digital resources, foster knowledge advancement, and prepare students for a digitalized society and working life. The fourth principle specifically adheres to the theoretical framing of transformative agency in Chapter 1.

1   *Generic digital competence* cuts across subject disciplines and specifies the general digital competence that educators and students need to function as active participants doing epistemic work in digitalized contexts. Such competence requires some instrumental skills, but more important is deep, conceptual understanding of the artifacts involved, the affordances that emerge, and how these relate to underlying and fundamental assumptions about learning and teaching. In addition, there are crucial ethical and societal issues that increasingly emerge as the boundaries between humans and nonhumans become blurred (see Chapter 8).

2   *Didactic digital competence* captures how scientific disciplines are affected and afforded by digitalization: representations, knowledge practices, communicative ecologies, etc. The brief discussion (above) of subject-specific implications has served as an introduction to a field that awaits further scholarly development. Also assessment practices need to be transformed, including tasks and criteria. Such issues are beyond the scope of the present volume, but will be briefly revisited in Chapter 8 (teaching as design).

3   *Professionally oriented digital competence* is connected to students' professional enactment of PDC: how they with educators codesign learning activities and environments, approach diverse types of assessment, and communicate with peers and other relevant parties. The point is to bridge current campus practices with (future) workplace practices. With the rapid turnover of what is considered valid knowledge and the permanent uncertainty of what the future holds and requires, students will continuously encounter a series of problem situations and challenges on how to transform them. Consequently, a fourth dimension is needed: transformative digital competence.

4   *Transformative digital competence* captures students' and educators' competence in taking initiatives and transforming their practices by selecting and using relevant digital tools. It arises as a necessity when agents are placed in demanding situations involving a conflict of motives, thus creating a wish or need to break out of the current situation. This is where transformative agency and the dynamic and dialectic relations between S1 and S2 are operationalized as competence indicators.

As mentioned previously, these principles do not represent a clean break with previous and existing competence frameworks. In line with TPACK, DigCompEdu, and the original PDC framework presented above, the principles highlight that PDC involves insight into how people learn, as well as how learning can be fostered, sustained, and made visible, but also discipline specific issues. Furthermore, it focuses on teachers as designers of digital learning environments and learning trajectories, an emergent competence vital for educators and students (Lund & Hauge, 2011). Unlike the SAMR model (with which we share and approve of the focus on expansion), the PDC framework is not sequential or hierarchic; rather, it should be seen as a cluster concept where reciprocity and multilevel efforts are required and with sensitivity towards social as well as epistemic context. There is a fine balance to be struck between preparing for uncertainty and transformation while offering guidelines and structure for epistemic development. However, we argue that such potential contradictions promote quality and development.

Notes

1 See the DigCompEdu 'check-in' at https://ec.europa.eu/eusurvey/runner/DigCompEdu-S-EN.
2 An overview and meta-analysis of 43 such frameworks can be found in Appendix 3 of the Professional Digital Competence Framework for Teachers (Kelentrić, Helland, & Arstorp, 2017): https://www.udir.no/contentassets/081d3aef2e4747b096387aba163691e4/pfdk-framework.pdf.

References

Bakhtin, M. M. (1979/2000). *The Dialogic Imagination. Four Essays by M.M. Bakhtin.* Austin: University of Texas Press.

Baptista, G., & Oliveira, T. (2019). Gamification and Serious Games: A Literature Meta-analysis and Integrative Model. *Computers in Human Behavior, 92*, 306–315.

Castells, M. (1996). *The Rise of the Network Society.* Cambridge, MA: Blackwell Publishers.

Castells, M. (1997). *The Power of Identity.* Malden, MA: Blackwell.

Castells, M. (1998). *End of Millennium.* Malden, MA: Blackwell Publishers.

Chai, C. S., Koh, J. H. L., & Tsai, C.-C. (2013). A Review of Technological Pedagogical Content Knowledge. *Educational Technology & Society, 16*(2), 31–51.

Cope, B., & Kalantzis, M. (Eds.). (2000). *Multiliteracies. Literacy Learning and the Design of Social Futures.* London; New York, NY: Routledge.

Engeström, Y. (1987). *Learning by Expanding: An Activity-Theoretical Approach to Developmental Research.* Helsinki: Orienta-Konsultit Oy.

Gee, J. P., Hull, G., & Lankshear, C. (1996). *The New Work Order: Behind the Language of the New Capitalism.* Sydney: Allen & Unwin.

Hamilton, E. R., Rosenberg, J. M., & Akcaoglu, M. (2016). The Substitution Augmentation Modification Redefinition (SAMR) Model: A Critical Review and Suggestions for Its Use. *TechTrends, 60*(5), 433–441. doi:10.1007/s11528-016-0091-y

Hearn, G. N., & Foth, M. (2007). Communicative Ecologies: Editorial Preface. *Electronic Journal of Communication, 17*(1–2). Retrieved from https://eprints.qut.edu.au/8171/1/8171.pdf

Ilomäki, L., Paavola, S., Lakkala, M., & Kantosalo, A. (2016). Digital Competence – An Emergent Boundary Concept for Policy and Educational Research. *Education and Information Technologies, 21*(3), 655–679. doi:10.1007/s10639-014-9346-4

Kaptelinin, V., & Nardi, B. A. (2006). *Acting with Technology: Activity Theory and Interaction Design.* Cambridge, MA; London: MIT Press.

Kelentrić, M., Helland, K., & Arstorp, A.-T. (2017). *Professional Digital Competence – Framework for Teachers.* Oslo: The Norwegian Centre for ICT in Education.

Koehler, M. J., & Mishra, P. (2009). What Is Technological Pedagogical Content Knowledge? *Contemporary Issues in Technology and Teacher Education, 9*(1), 60–70.

Lankshear, C., Snyder, I., & Green, B. (2000). *Teachers and Technoliteracy: Managing Literacy, Technology and Learning in Schools.* St Leonards NSW: Allen & Unwin.

Lehtinen, E. (2010). The Potential of Teaching and Learning Supported by ICT for the Acquisition of Deep Conceptual Knowledge and the Development of Wisdom. In E. De Corte & J. E. Fenstad (Eds.), *From Information to Knowledge; from Knowledge to Wisdom: Challenges and Changes Facing Higher Education in the Digital Age* (pp. 79–88). London: Portland Press.

Ludvigsen, S., Lund, A., Rasmussen, I., & Säljö, R. (Eds.). (2010). *Learning across Sites; New Tools, Infrastructures and Practices.* London; New York, NY: Routledge.

Lund, A. (2016). I Am Connected, Therefore I Am: Polycontextual Bridging in Education. In E. Elstad (Ed.), *Educational Technology and Polycontextual Bridging* (pp. 129–145). Rotterdam, NL: SENSE Publishers.

Lund, A., Furberg, A., Bakken, J., & Engelien, K. (2014). What Does Professional Digital Competence Mean in Teacher Education? *Nordic Journal of Digital Literacy, 9*(4), 281–299.

Lund, A., & Hauge, T. E. (2011). Designs for Teaching and Learning in Technology Rich Learning Environments. *Nordic Journal of Digital Literacy, 6*(4), 258–271.

Lund, A., & Rasmussen, I. (2008). The Right Tool for the Wrong Task? Match and Mismatch between First and Second Stimulus in Double Stimulation. *International Journal of Computer-Supported Collaborative Learning, 3*(4), 25–51.

Mishra, P., & Koehler, M. J. (2006). Technological Pedagogical Content Knowledge: A Framework for Teacher Knowledge. *Teachers College Record, 108*(6), 1017–1054.

Puentedura, R. (2006). Transformation, Technology, and Education [Blog post]. Retrieved from http://hippasus.com/resources/tte/

Redecker, C. (2017). *European Framework for the Digital Competence of Educators: DigCompEdu* (No. JRC107466). Joint Research Centre (Seville site).

Shulman, L. S. (1986). Those Who Understand: Knowledge Growth in Teaching. *Educational Researcher, 15*, 4–21.

Shulman, L. S. (1987). Knowledge and Teaching: Foundations of the New Reform. *Harvard Educational Review, 57*, 1–22.

Stetsenko, A. (2017). *The Transformative Mind. Expanding Vygotsky's Approach to Development and Education.* New York, NY: Cambridge University Press.

Voogt, J., Fisser, P., Pareja Roblin, N., Tondeur, J., & van Braakt, J. (2013). Technological Pedagogical Content Knowledge – A Review of the Literature. *Journal of Computer Assisted Learning, 29*(2), 109–121. doi:10.1111/j.1365-2729.2012.00487.x

Vygotsky, L. S. (1978). *Mind in Society: The Development of Higher Psychological Processes.* Cambridge, MA: Harvard University Press.

Yamagata-Lynch, L. (2010). *Activity Systems Analysis Methods. Understanding Complex Learning Environments.* New York, NY; Dordrecht; Heidelberg; London: Springer.

7 Transforming teacher education – analysis of transformative initiatives

Throughout Chapters 1–6, we have sought to conceptualize digitalization and professional digital competence (PDC) from an epistemic perspective involving transformation and going beyond existing educational practices. Also, we have sought to connect such efforts to a notion of quality and how people can make reasoned judgments as to what amounts to quality practices, anchored in scientific criteria and fundamental assumptions of learning and development, in our case elicited from sociocultural and cultural–historical perspectives.

In this chapter, we make an empirical turn. As observed by, e.g., the Organization for Economic Cooperation and Development (OECD), "Solving non-routine problems is a key competence in a world full of changes, uncertainty and surprise where we strive to achieve so many ambitious goals" (Csapó & Funke, 2017). This calls for competences we have subsumed under the PDC umbrella but so far operationalized to lesser extent. Therefore, in this chapter, we present and analyze efforts from two selected Norwegian universities that aim to promote and foster PDC of teacher educators and student teachers.

Analytically, we approach the efforts of fostering PDC as case studies (Yin, 2009). Case studies afford deep and nuanced understandings of particular situations; in our context how an educational program is transformed to make it more relevant for the working life and digitalized society students will encounter. Case studies might produce unanticipated results as the case unfolds and bring about fresh research agendas. These characteristics align with our focus on expansion, transformative agency, and going beyond the status quo.

A risk with case studies is context-specific findings with low general interest, unless the cases are carefully selected. We have chosen the two cases based on deliberate, information-oriented selection. The cases and vignettes that are introduced should be considered as 'revelatory' and not as empirical evidence. They are revelatory as they represent a hitherto under-researched phenomenon (Yin, 2009), in this case developing PDC at micro and meso levels.

An aspect that makes Norwegian teacher education (TE) particularly interesting, is that teachers are required to enact research-based professional practices and make split decisions and negotiate thorny situations not only from experience or 'gut feeling' but from research-informed insights (Munthe & Rogne, 2015). We will focus on *what may be* (trends) and *what could be* (visions of an ideal) (Schofield, 1993). Thus, they serve as "fuzzy prediction (…) which can serve as a guide to professional action" (Bassey, 2010, p. 5).

Further, TE is an interesting case because it is put under particular pressure to adapt and transform educational practices to the needs of a digital age. Thus, the dual commitment described in Chapter 6 is very clear. Murray and Male (2005) call them 'second order teachers' because they educate students who later will become teachers to other students. Therefore, they are expected to be good role models, by, e.g., exploring and using different digital technologies, stimulate students to reflect upon what characterizes appropriate use, and promote awareness of how different epistemological "points of departure" can influence teachers' use of digital technology. "As second-order practitioners teacher educators induct their students into the practices and discourses of both school teaching and teacher education" (Murray & Male, 2005, p. 126). However, preparing students for lifelong learning in technology-rich work life contexts, e.g., is relevant across quantum physics, ancient Greek, nursing, engineering, history, economics, etc. Thus, what we learn from a case study of TE might be valuable across programs. This does not imply that findings can easily be transferred; rather, it makes a case for analytical generalization, i.e., "the extent to which findings from one study can be used as a guide to what might occur in another situation" (Kvale, 1996, p. 233). Such analytical generalization rests on a presumption that the phenomena and data we examine are more than examples. They are empirical carriers of deeper principles of digitalization and educational transformation.

Despite analytical generalizability, the intention is also to illustrate how the concepts and theoretical anchoring introduced in the book can be applied when observing, analyzing, and discussing institutional efforts to transform and go beyond the status quo.

Case 1: PDC and transformative agency in a small private online community

The Department of Teacher Education and School Research (DTESR) at the University of Oslo has for several years sought to foster PDC among student teachers as well as faculty. With its staff of approximately 140 (including a small but very competent group of engineers with a combination of digital and pedagogical expertise) and more than 1,000 students, it counts as Norway's largest teacher educating body and is of considerable size also by international standards. The DTESR hosts four research groups, Norway's first center for excellence in TE, Center for Professional Learning in Teacher Education (ProTed), and the Quality in Nordic Teaching (QUINT) center for excellence in research. The implication is that development, change, and transformation challenge not only what may be established practices but the sheer volume of the organization where these are cultivated.

About DTESR

DTESR does not fit into the 'Jurassic Park' category we invoked in Chapter 1. First, a number of researchers at the DTESR and the Faculty of Education had from the late 1990s researched connections between digitalization, learning, and teaching. This resulted in context-specific contributions, especially on the use of collaborative technologies and collaborative learning in schools but also on teachers as designers of technology-rich learning environments and activities (see, e.g., Lund, 2008; Lund & Hauge, 2011). Second, the conceptualization of PDC presented in Chapter 6 made teacher educators aware that digitalization in TE was severely inadequate and mostly the responsibility of individual 'beacons'. Third, and partly as a result of this recognition, powerful and principled local initiatives to connect digitalization and deeper issues of HE and TE materialized in future-oriented projects.

One example was efforts to constitute a new 'exam ecology' that challenged the entire exam mind-set and enactment. DTESR broke out of a situation we earlier have referred to as an S1, a problem situation that represents a conflict of motives or contradictory state of affairs. The University of Oslo wanted to 'digitalize' all exams. For DTESR the question was whether to stick to well-proven practices and merely digitalize these in order to meet new demands with minimal effort or break away and expand into exam practices that better match the epistemological dimensions of digitalization and recent educational research. The latter option represented notably higher risks and more work for faculty and administrators, including the technology staff. However, the DTESR opted for the latter and – to cut a long story short – developed a 'digitalized exam' that was presented to students at the start of the term, built on the following principles:

a   *Assignment.* On the day of the exam, students are presented to video clip from an authentic classroom. Based on this, they develop a problem statement that takes a subject-specific, pedagogical, didactic, or experiential point of departure. The competence to be documented is to what extent they manage to juxtapose, combine, and discuss different knowledge types as they examine the video case and synthesize their analysis.

b   *Available resources.* Although there are no restrictions, no specific resources are provided or recommended (beyond what is being part of the program).

c   *Student activities.* Students are responsible for the submitted exam paper as individuals, but can solve it in collaboration from any preferred location. Time pressure (four hours) requires that they be well prepared and prevent that collaboration replace individual commitment. All through the exam, technical help is available.

d   *Assessment.* Analyses of the exam papers are done with a view to how the student teachers managed to make use of, align, and reach conclusions and syntheses with explanatory power for their problem statement. Nearly all – admittedly to various extent – integrated diverse knowledge (theory, field experiences, subject-specific problems, etc.) when they examined the case (see Vestøl & Lund (2017) for an extended discussion).

The exam experience could in itself qualify as a case study of transformative agency, breaking out of a tradition (exams, assessment) where there was a conflict of motives. Should exams provide data that could be measured and graded, or should it be an opportunity for learning under a certain pressure? This S1 was sought suspended by putting available resources (S2) to work: research-based pedagogy, digital affordances, and social interaction. In this context, transformative agency and the double stimulation principle were operationalized on a program level. The outcome was an exam with a more pronounced student focus where juxtaposing and drawing on diverse knowledge types amounted to expanding the exam format and making it more valid for 21st-century epistemic and work-related practices.

Developing PDC in teacher education

In 2016, the DTESR introduced a modern learning management system (LMS) which supported the Learning Tools Interoperability (LTI) standard. Supporting such a standard implies that the LMS structure invites users to include a plethora of different apps. At DTESR the LMS architecture encouraged collaborative and adaptive learning, sharing of resources, video conferencing, learning analytics, and the use of relevant third-party software and mobile apps. Consequently, a small private online course (SPOC) was developed. In the following case, practices and experiences from learning practices in this SPOC are in focus. Thus, the main focus is at micro level.

The SPOC was developed and integrated in a master's program in TE, where practicum, research and development (R&D) competence, and PDC were presented as longitudinal themes throughout the program. Historically, workshops on basic software had been given, which gradually developed into courses where the use of LMSs was essential. Issues that dealt with learning, teaching, and epistemological implications were introduced in lectures and sometimes discussed with students in seminars. However, it is fair to say that until 2015, digitalization in TE tended to be instrumental and was treated more as an *ad hoc* component than an educational and epistemological force with fundamental implications for practice.

In 2016, new and mandatory assignments were introduced in the master program. For instance, students should design and share a technology-rich learning environment with activities, write, and publish a reflection note based on digital experiences during practicum where research-based knowledge also was integrated, and they should connect subject-specific features to digital representations. Everything was shared and made accessible in the SPOC.

In the following, we examine how student teachers faced and responded to PDC tasks and assignments in their sixth semester. The data were collected from an online survey, digital traces in the SPOC, and a series of focus group interviews with students. An extended presentation, analysis and discussion is published elsewhere (Brevik, Gudmundsdottir, Lund, & Strømme, 2019). In this chapter, we demonstrate principles underlying the tasks and assignments and how the students responded to such challenges, and with the PDC outlined in Chapter 6 as the conceptual framework.

For our analysis, we return to the principles of double stimulation and transformative agency introduced in Chapter 1. In line with the overall purpose of this volume, we focus on the epistemic work involved when digitalization meets HE. Specifically, we turn to situations where student teachers face complex challenges that involve a fundamental problem which escapes obvious solutions. They often pose a critical conflict or dilemma, demand choosing between incompatible alternatives, and tend to leave the agent(s) with conflicting motives or an impasse. This also involves uncertainty and risk-taking; students can become agents of their own learning and development, but they cannot predict all consequences of the process. Such situations are increasingly typical in learning as well as future work (Facer, 2011). How students come to terms with, respond to, break out of, or expand their repertoire as a result of an S1 can be studied by analyzing which resources they invoke: epistemic (disciplinary knowing), discursive (conceptual, metaphorical), social (peers, experts), and material (digital, analog).

In the following, we will present vignettes that demonstrate what transformative agency entails, how it can be studied, and how student teachers expand or transform their educational repertoire. They should be approached and understood in the context of the TE program's wider aim (an 'overarching S1') to develop student teachers' PDC. They are not chosen to demonstrate a 'successful' transformative agency but because they show the diversity of S1 and in ways students struggle with these as they pick up and appropriate a series of resources (S2) in order to overcome their challenges.

Vignette 1: *integrating different knowledge types*

One persistent challenge in HE (and education in general) is to integrate academic and experiential knowledge (Jenset, Klette, & Hammerness, 2018; Lund & Eriksen, 2016) so that the two are mutually constitutive for knowledge advancement and taking on complex problems. This is an especially relevant issue for professional education (nursing, engineering, law, etc.), but no scientific discipline (theoretical physics also depend on a dialogue with nature) can be reduced to one knowledge category only. For student teachers, integrating knowledge types also pertains to their own designs of classroom activities. One focus group discussed this issue as they designed a lesson plan together, involving the use of digital technologies to support their pupils' learning processes in school. In their designs, the student teachers needed to integrate different knowledge types (subject-specific, pedagogical, didactic, and experiential) and justify such designs by drawing on theoretical perspectives. At the same time, they recognized that knowledge advancement was potentially threatened or replaced by the more entertaining and recreational features in some digital applications. As Olivia observed,

> It is very good that we had such an assignment, because when you have to justify using literature, you do not just plan instruction to be fun ... I think it is somewhat easy to fall into pitfalls when designing digital instruction: "Oh, this is fun for the students; they can just relax and have some fun", and then you lose the outcomes they are expected to have.

Potential conflict is also recognized by fellow student Astrid:

> I absolutely agree with that ... This is maybe one of the things I find most successful regarding the integration of pedagogy, subject didactics and the [SPOC] really, almost throughout the entire semester. ... But at the same time, there was a very strong encouragement to use digital tools as much as possible. So I think it was very good to see how you could use all three aspects [pedagogy, subject didactics and the PDC SPOC] ... So we used quite a few digital tools and such, but I think perhaps that was some of the finest; that we got the combination of all three.

Another student, Lisa expresses similar reflections on digitalization and collaboration:

> The group assignment is the one thing that really helped me in understanding how all that knowledge on digital tools can be utilized in teaching. But without CANVAS [i.e. the SPOC], my group would not have used Padlets, TalkWall or such [digital tools]. Seventy percent of our group assignment was from one place or another in CANVAS ... Working with CANVAS has given me an increased scope that I could not have gained through lectures about digital tools, since I need to work and Experiment with these tools on my own.

Olivia's situation can be seen as a potentially critical conflict – the temptation of merely using digital resources for fun, obscuring the learning object(s). She demonstrates embryonic transformative agency as she seeks to avoid such pitfalls when designing lessons. Astrid operationalizes Olivia's emergent transformative agency by highlighting the collaborative aspect of the group assignment and its ability to integrate pedagogy, didactics, and the SPOC (S2). This aspect becomes evident as she talks in the plural (i.e., "we"). Hence, Astrid demonstrates more developed transformative agency in acknowledging both the value of integration and the collaborative efforts of designing technology-based lessons. Together, Astrid's and Olivia's reflections might be seen as envisioning new models for future practices (Haapasaari & Kerosuo, 2015). Lisa acknowledges the increased need to understand how theoretical knowledge can be productively used in teaching. She argues that the SPOC helped them find new ways of using digital tools, and the group assignment in the seminars helped her develop this understanding, i.e., envisioning new models (Haapasaari & Kerosuo, 2015). Lisa demonstrates transformative agency as she recognizes a series of S2 in terms of SPOC resources and seminar assignments influencing her PDC.

In sum, this vignette demonstrates how students take on a persistent and critical challenge in TE: the integration of diverse knowledge types, domains, and resources.

Vignette 2: bridging in-school and out-of-school contexts

This vignette is linked to the thorny issue of continuation or discontinuation of educational practices inside and outside of educational institutions, and how digitalization might facilitate bridging between the two contexts, i.e., an extended learning environment (Lund, 2016). One of the assignments in the SPOC explicitly addressed this problem situation (S1) in English subject didactics: Many students demonstrate proficiency in English outside formal educational contexts, but this competence does not seem to be activated or carry value inside formal education (Brevik, 2016; Sundquist & Olin-Scheler, 2013).

The student teachers could access research articles on the problems of bridging educational practices across contexts. Then they were asked to design an educational activity (lesson) that might alleviate this problem situation (S1). This S1 represents a situation that is relatively new but increasingly common and – at least in our case – had not received much attention in TE. As this type of S1 is challenging for teachers responsible for meeting the curriculum while also keeping the individual pupil in mind, they often find themselves perplexed and immobilized (Lund, 2016). Thus, the assignment was designed to encourage student teachers to enact transformative agency by addressing this lack of bridging (S1) and to explicate new digital possibilities (S2) in their English teaching.

Student teacher Julie exercised agency by first seeking out and interviewing pupils: "The pupil I talked to said that he reads English outside of school when he plays video games, reads news and watches videos on YouTube". Based on the information, Julie proceeded by developing a teaching design involving a video game, seeking to bridge the pupil's lifeworld and the curriculum:

> I would use one video game, for example Fallout [a post-nuclear role playing game]. It could also serve as a good base to create a role play about a topic more connected to the curriculum. I have found some examples of role play with an historic context which can be used as a model to make my own role plays that serve the teaching of what I want them to learn.

Sharing this plan with her peers (and teachers) in the SPOC, Julie continued by discussing her design and how it serves to address larger, didactic issues:

> I will first talk about the digital role playing games, that they really are a great learning platform if used with purpose, and compare them with analog role playing. This lesson will serve as a final part of a bigger project.

Thus, we see how Julie explicates new educational possibilities. New educational affordances arise from linking the relevance of pupils' personal experiences to the English curriculum (first S2) and taking consequential actions to change her practice by designing a games-based English lesson, using the *Fallout* role-playing game (second S2).

Similarly, another student teacher, Peter, argues in the SPOC how he will update himself on the digital lives of young learners, adopting a future-oriented stance:

> In the future, I will try to develop my PDC by continually updating myself on the digital lives of young learners. Thus, I will be able to prepare my teaching in more engaging ways. I want to be an updated teacher who does not lag behind. I feel that this course has opened the doors to a universe I look forward to getting to know better, and it has taught me more about where I can and should seek knowledge.

Fellow students chime in on future-oriented and transformative perspectives. As Victoria observes,

> It would have been really cool if we had been challenged more often (…) encouraging us to be active in relation to various situations where we meet digital technologies would have been smart,

and some kind of motivation for us, and a good way to learn. (...)
So dare to be, kind of, a little like, 'Hooray! Today, let's play online games'.

By emphasizing the need for assignments where they had to be more active, the student teachers demonstrate how the SPOC assignment challenged them to expand on existing practices and develop transformative
agency. This vignette demonstrates how student teachers develop practices by encountering a demanding S1 and respond by bridging students' English competence in and out of school by doing epistemic work
mediated by digital resources. They engage in consequential actions to
develop their PDC and demonstrate how PDC is enacted in practice
when the corresponding resources (S2) are set in motion.

Vignette 3: committing to research-based approaches

TE (and HE in general) is expected and even required to be research
based, and very much so in Norway (Munthe & Rogne, 2015). This requires student engagement of a type that has not always been fostered
in TE. Thus, the final vignette is devoted to how student teachers cope
with an S1 that juxtaposes research and experiential knowledge.

The SPOC offered a module on "ICT and Learning: What Does
Research Say?", including hyperlinks to scholarly journals. Student
teachers were asked to search for research papers, summarize the methods, list findings, and assess the relevance for teaching and/or PDC
development. Digital traces in the SPOC illustrate tensions and opportunities articulated by the student teachers when assessing the relevance of
research papers. Space does not permit the full range of issues touched
upon by the students, but Arne invokes broader perspectives:

> The understanding of literacies from [Paolo] Freire [Brazilian
> educator and philosopher famous for promoting critical and
> emancipatory pedagogy] is of utmost importance for school as a
> formative project (...) It is relevant for a teacher to prepare pupils
> for multimodality ... so that they can become 'free citizens' in a
> multimodal world. To transfer his [Freire's] concept of literacy to
> media literacy is a significant step (...) If schools can appreciate
> such multimodal competence, it will embolden those who may not
> find the traditional notion of text to be satisfactory.

In the excerpt above, we see indications of how the student link research
to broader societal issues. This is an aspect of the overarching S1,

reflecting on how research extends the notion of PDC beyond instrumental skills. However, we also find students who struggle to see how research is related to teaching competence. For example, Maria claimed that finding and summarizing a research paper was "meaningless". Another said that "It [the research perspective] was so far removed from my life world". Ole makes an intriguing juxtaposition between instant use value and long-term professional development:

> I found it difficult to see how it [a research article] could be used in relation to my pupils. It is probably more like you [addressing a fellow student] touched upon when you brought up 'the teacher with the researcher's eye' ... then it could be extremely interesting ... I would really have liked to use it [the article] but not ... because this felt like 'you should apply this to the pupils and how the pupils can use it'. So, it was, like, I get the idea but ... I do not see myself reading it closely during placement periods thinking 'this is something I will use right now.

The above utterances demonstrate that conflicts of interest exist among the student teachers. Maria and Ole express resistance to using research. For them, turning to research does not represent breaking out of a situation, and they do not see the immediate relevance of research for their practices – neither for their own "life world", or Ole's pupils. Another concern is the temporal dimension. Ole sees no connection between the assignment and the school practice, which takes place simultaneously. However, taking up another student's expression of "the teacher with the researcher's eye", he acknowledges the more strategic value of research-based resources, representing a potential S2 for breaking out of a constrained role and expanding into a research-based profession.

Synthesizing

Taken together, the vignettes reflect the rhythm and flow of collaboratively enacted transformative agency in order to bring students' PDC to fruition. The process is riddled with tensions, uncertainties, and conflict of motives inherent in the problem situations (Sannino, 2015). However, analysis of the total data corpus (Brevik et al., 2019) reveals certain patterns that amount to PDC via phases (not necessarily stepwise) of transformative agency. First, student teachers develop PDC through prefiguring new models enacting their expertise (i.e., critiquing, explicating, and envisioning). Second, they develop PDC by taking consequential actions (i.e., explicating, envisioning, committing to actions, and taking actions). Third, they develop PDC by committing to research-based actions (resisting, criticizing, explicating, envisioning, and committing to actions). These patterns are, thus, not mere illustrations and were not selected because they demonstrate 'successful' transformation, but because they show these patterns through conflicting motives, differences of opinion, and diverse reflections from the student teachers (see Haapasaari, Engeström, & Kerosuo, 2014; Haapasaari & Kerosuo, 2015, for relevant studies on transformative agency).

So far, we have followed the development of PDC as it materialized on micro levels – students (and to some extent, HE teachers) designing and engaging in interactions conducive to fostering PDC. While it should tell us something about possible approaches to advancing PDC in HE, we need to add an institutional perspective to capture the totality of what is at stake and how HE institutions might cope.

Case 2: the LUDO project

This case is a process study of a large, ongoing R&D initiative called LUDO, focusing on learning and education in a digital age. The main aim of the project is to redesign TE to ensure that all students develop PDC and are prepared for being teachers in technology-rich classrooms. The project is located at a Norwegian multicampus university. The case is special in the sense that it invites us to capture transformation and digitalization in HE as the process unfolds. This provides a unique 'lived' experience to the case, something which we believe will resonate with the many academics and professionals experiencing fundamental changes in their workplace.

This case study (Yin, 2018) is inspired by action-based research (Somekh, 2005). Typically, the aim of such research is to develop knowledge and understand a phenomenon involving transformation through interventions. Here, the approach is used to develop theoretical and experiential understanding about how educational quality in the shape of PDC can be fostered. Compared with, for instance, design-based research, action-based research emphasizes the practical dimensions of the intervention and engages, to a greater extent, the teachers or practitioners as active partners in the study. Consequently, action-based research is sometimes promoted as democratic (Nielsen & Nielsen, 2015). Practitioner participation is also similar to the formative interventions approach developed by the Helsinki Developmental Work Research (DVR) and Change Laboratory (Engeström, 2011). With its emphasis on agency, transformation, and ecological validity (correspondence with an unpredictable and serendipitous context), the DVR principles are in many ways a methodological counterpart to the conceptual framework used in this volume.

The focus in action research and DVR is both on conducting interventions and investigating the outcomes of the activities that follow. Two perspectives are continuously invoked: the 'emic' (interpretations from within) by the participants (including the project leader/researcher) and the 'etic' (external) view. In LUDO the etic view is held outside the university by additional researchers who have been engaged in developing surveys, conducting interviews, and assessing the project.

About LUDO

With the LUDO project, the University of South-Eastern Norway was, after a national call, funded with 2,1m EUR to develop a future-oriented TE that prepares students for work in digital environments. The project lasts three years from April 1, 2018, until March 31, 2021.

It has become common for schools to equip each student with an iPad, PC, or Chromebook. In this way, students gain access to enormous amounts of information, activities, and communication and interaction arenas. As highlighted in several places of this book, the digital resources can potentially be used to engage students in learning, to make teaching and tasks in schools relevant for the society we live in, and adapt learning to the diversity of students by selecting digital resources based on their interests and potential. However, this calls for teachers who can scaffold and guide the students while they actively try to solve tasks, who know how to help children and young people steer clear of both the social and educational pitfalls (mindless surfing, plagiarism, cyberbullying, etc.). Also, we need teachers with an overview of which digital and analog resources that seem appropriate to include in different learning situations. They also need to know how to teach students to identify credible information, cite sources, protect their own intellectual property, apply ethical values and attitudes in communication and interaction, produce their own digital resources, and reflect upon their own and others' actions in digital contexts. A daunting endeavor, indeed.

With LUDO, the university takes initiatives to make sure that the student teachers will be well prepared for taking the role and responsibility described above. The institution develops program plans and facilitates the development of teacher educators' PDC together with teachers in schools. The project involves four campuses and the practice field from a large region. The diversity and complexity give access to social, material, and epistemic resources, which the project strives to combine and take advantage of.

As indicated in case 1, combining knowledge types while operationalizing and developing PDC can be challenging, not just for students. Basing development on merely experiential knowledge soon reduces education to an instrumental activity. On the other hand, it is often demanding to immediately see the practical relevance of research-based knowledge. Hence, LUDO has searched for ways to bridge the many diverse but equally relevant knowledge types. Still, as Hoholm (2009) asserts, innovation is typically observed if heterogeneous elements are made into more durable patterns. But such 'quilting' cannot be sufficiently managed by single actors with clear goals; it is often the result of multiple interacting actors with unclear, multiple, and conflicting interests and goals. This calls for co-construction work as illustrated in Figure 7.1.

These three categories of agents (teacher educators from HE and schools and student teachers) each add rich access to a broad range of knowledge types (experiential, academic, subject specific, etc., i.e., S2) that, when combined, potentially make TE offer the best conditions for developing PDC among their students and teachers.

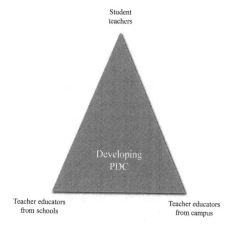

Figure 7.1 Co-constructing PDC: diverse agents and knowledge contexts.

Vignette 1: seed projects

The triangle (Figure 7.1) is operationalized in several settings. First, LUDO supports "seed projects" initiated by teachers from campus, who have produced ideas about how PDC can be developed in specific subjects. All projects involve students and teacher educators from schools. In one seed-project, the triangle amounted to a research community seeking to bridge personal experiences with more societal concerns as to how digital technologies can be used to promote democratic participation in education. The seed-project participants discuss what 'democratic didactics' is, explore different digital resources that can enhance democracy in education, and discuss values and challenges that emerge when research-based knowledge is integrated with experiential knowledge. The S1 they encounter is the challenging question of how digital technologies can be used to enhance democratic education. The research community and participants' different knowledge types add up to a series of S2. The expansive efforts of breaking out of the stifling S1 amount to how digital resources can be activated in order to merge knowledge types and logics. Thus, PDC outstrips technocentric or instrumental approaches and moves into sociopolitical and ethical waters.

All projects are obliged to make plans for how knowledge that develops in the LUDO project can be shared in the institution. In this case, the knowledge that develops will be introduced to all student teachers and shared across campuses through, for instance, episodes about democracy (as indicated above) in LUDO's proprietary podcasts. Such efforts serve to make the S1 ↔ S2 dialectics shared and sustainable in the organization.

Another S1 that probably many readers of this book will recognize is when a group of students is hard to engage in reading and discussing research literature. A seed project seeks to overcome this S1 by exploring how digital technologies can be used to promote students' engagement. Students and a teacher from a school and together with the teacher educators from campus and selected students approached the problem situation by introducing a new type of assignment, potentially an S2: Before class, students produce short videos where they summarize what they have read, highlight particular meaningful or challenging issues, and raise questions they want to discuss with peers and their teachers. The video clips are shared and give the teachers and the class substantive knowledge about students' reading, topics of interest, and questions they have. Selected videos are used in class, often as a springboard for the remainder of the lesson. In this case, to break out of the S1, the particular assignment was introduced as a potential S2. It builds on a well-known motivation principle – that people tend to engage in tasks when their effort is observed, taken into account, and appreciated by others (see, for instance, Ryan & Deci, 2000).

Vignette 2: employing teachers from schools in teacher education

Another well-known challenge (S1) for HE is developing programs that are both research based and relevant for work practices the programs qualify for. In many countries, HE has for the last decades been pushed towards prioritizing research (Aldersley, 1995). For professional programs, like teacher education, this implies that, when teacher educators are employed, candidates with research merits are prioritized before candidates with practical experience. Thus, different knowledge types carry unequal value. To suspend such asymmetry (an S1), the field has seen initiatives such as tighter and more reciprocal collaboration between HE and the practice field and 'split' positions where people work across academic and practice contexts (Lillejord & Børte, 2014). LUDO collaborates with four municipalities and employs teachers from schools in 20 per cent positions whose tasks at the university are to collaborate with teacher educators from campus on designing, conducting, and evaluating lessons, and provide students with educational experiences and perspectives that prepare them well for being teachers in a digital age. This amounts to a series of S2.

To illustrate how such collaboration unfolds, we draw the attention to one particular teacher, John (name changed). He is a teacher who works across contexts and thereby develops polycontextual competency (Lund, 2016). He runs a learning laboratory located in the competence center in one of the involved municipalities, and Johns' 20 per cent position at the university implies that he, on average, collaborates one day every week with teacher educators from the campus and student teachers who are located close to the laboratory. The rest of the week he supports kindergarten staff and kids, school leaders, teachers, pupils, and others to work innovatively with a repertoire of digital technologies.

A teacher educator from campus, Lisa, characterizes the collaboration with John saying that

> It is characterized by the fact that it is not institutionalized. Not in the sense that the leaders don't care about the development, they really do, but in the sense that we are all faced with a challenge that is

new. The theme [PDC], the concepts, the educational practices that develop are new to all parties. The room [the learning lab] is new and people talk about the competencies of the future there. So, in a way, one starts from scratch as collaborators ... with no expectations of how the collaboration should be. Everything is new! This invites us to think innovatively together. In previous collaboration with the field of practice, we have been sitting in meeting after meeting with the principals and teachers from school ... we have been sitting a lot and it has resulted in few "doings". At the learning lab we, of course, have meetings to make plans, but the way from plans to action is very short - we don't like to just talk, we like to act!

I think that people who are engaged in digital technology use and learning often tend to share some basic perspectives on learning; they value creativity, the power of innovation, the desire to try out new things. We do not sit around a table, almost never.

Statements like this are not systematically gathered for the purpose of doing research and might be very context specific. Nevertheless, such statements indicate how transforming processes unfold. Lisa's statement carries insight into a unique 'lived' experience from the case and that might be recognizable across contexts. She also expands a personal experience into a collective perspective: "Everything is new! This invites us to think innovatively together".

In this vignette, the epistemological practices that develop seem to become more 'performative' (Säljö, 2010), not just documenting knowledge and competence but demonstrating how this is developed in collaborative activity. Lisa's statement indicates that the novelty, the learning laboratory as space, and the presence of polycontextual competence, a series of S2, trigger teacher educators from campus and teacher educators from schools to collaborate in more performative ways: "We do not sit around a table, almost never". Observations from educational activities where games, virtual reality, programming, and drones are used, together with the project's blog, add to this impression. As the project is unfolding, one very important research issue is to pursue and document the intensity, generalizability, and sustainability of such efforts that aim to connect academic and practical knowledge for performative purposes.

Vignette 3: from micro initiatives to institutional change

When institutions want to innovate, for instance, by creating programs where knowledge from research and working life aims to prepare students for future work practices, they are in for a dual challenge. On the one hand, they need to engage particularly qualified and interested individuals in micro initiatives like seed projects; on the other hand, they simultaneously need to involve the whole institution in the project in order to promote sustainable change. This amounts to contextual sensitivity. In order to be as context sensitive as possible, project status is systematically evaluated throughout the project, and planned interventions are calibrated or changed based on the data from these evaluations. The project initiatives and ensuing evaluations acknowledge the presence of controversies in innovation (Engeström, 1987; Hoholm, 2009). Our aim is, in line with Hoholm (2009, p. 33), to understand "what dynamics produce and fuel the inherent tensions of innovation processes. What are they, how do they influence the process, and how is the settling of conflicts enabled or hindered?" Such questions invoke similarities to the problem situations (S1) we have discussed in Chapter 1 and in the previous case of this chapter, only now we focus more on the institutional level.

One important instrument for raising context sensitivity was a survey developed and conducted in collaboration with four other universities and the Nordic Institute for Studies in Innovation, Research and Education (NIFU). The main aim was to map and analyze teacher educators' efforts to enhance their own and their students' PDC. Two hundred and ninety-one teacher educators from five universities and university colleges participated. The results show that teacher educators experience that digitalization promotes new pedagogical and didactic methods, gives increased access to and sharing of academic knowledge, and changes the teacher role (Daus, Aamodt & Tømte, 2019). Ninety-two per cent of the respondents to some or a great extent teaches students about the importance of being critical to digital sources and how to use sources right. Seventy-eight per cent focuses on how to use digital resources in diverse task types, and seventy-two per cent teaches students about copyright. Participants paid less attention to social challenges that emerge in digital environments. Fifty-five per cent either to a small extent or never focuses on how to prevent, uncover, and deal with cyberbullying, offensive, or other unwanted language or incidents when they educate student teachers. Sixty-five per cent either to a small extent or never say they work with how to prevent digital activities that distract students or how to teach in classes where each student has his/her own digital device. Forty-one per cent is neutral or disagree with the statement that "digital development changes the content of the subjects".

The percentages invoke a picture of an educational program with great awareness towards, e.g., the need to approach digital sources critically and who are sensitive to how such sources could be used right. However, it does not come across as digitally 'seduced' or operating at the digital frontier when it comes to how digitalization impacts on social and epistemological practices and challenges fundamental assumptions concerning what students need to learn in subjects. A closer look at the data shows that the institutions are heterogeneous and that teacher educators' expectations and practices regarding digitalization vary from enthusiasts to noncommitment.

From an epistemological point of view, it is particularly interesting to note that digitalization seems to impact more on how teacher educators educate students than the content in TE. Looking closer at what teacher educators use digital technologies for, the survey shows that ninety-six per cent to some or great extent use ICT to communicate and correspond with students, ninety-five per cent to present students for content in class, ninety-one per cent to assess students' tasks, and eighty-one per cent to supervise students when they solve tasks. Eighty-six per cent use digital technologies to visualize or simulate subject-specific content. The high percentages indicate a positive approach to digitalization for teaching and supervision practices. It might be that the most positive and interested teacher educators might have answered the survey, whereas the more noncommitted or even resistant have not.

The survey indicates that teacher educators are willing to explore and use different digital technologies in education. Still, they spend less time on stimulating students to reflect upon how digitalization comes with epistemological implications. Few use digital technologies to 'flip' education, promote discussions in subjects, make teaching more relevant for working life, or collaborate with schools. If teachers are expected to educate students in different subjects and develop their competencies, but also to be good role models ("second order teachers", Murray & Male, 2005), the digital practices educators develop need to be highly relevant. So, how do we deal with the fact that 35 per cent of the respondents to a small extent or never facilitate students' reflections on what digital development means for their professional practice?

The informants consider themselves as average at facilitating the development of student teachers' PDC. However, ambitions for teachers' digital competence are high and digital technologies change rapidly. Daus, Aamodt, and Tømte (2019) therefore argue that teacher educators need continuous development. The teacher educators in the survey report that they mainly develop their digital skills by exploring digital technologies on their own. Some collaborate with colleagues, but attending courses is rarely reported. The respondents from the university referred to in the LUDO project report that they have a clearer focus on PDC compared to the respondents from the other universities who participated in the survey.

In LUDO we have ought to combine what we have called vertical initiatives (like seed projects) with horizontal initiatives that are designed for the wide community of teacher educators. For instance, last year the university decided to spend three full days, distributed over the academic year, on the theme PDC. Critical discussions were an aim, and the entire staff from TE was invited to all-day seminars together with selected students as well as teacher educators from schools. Researchers engaged in formative dialogue research joined the group of project members and experts who planned the seminars and systematically observed the discussions that emerged. Each seminar was followed up through debriefings aiming to understand the dynamics that produced and fueled the tensions of the interventions that were initiated (Engeström, 1987; Hoholm, 2009).

The first seminar was an introduction to how knowledge work changes with digitalization, followed by discussions in subject-specific groups about what PDC is, how it best can be developed in and through the subject, and what support colleagues needed in order to foster PDC among themselves. Feedback during the discussions frequently expressed a wish to explore digital practices further and share more experiences. Therefore, the second seminar contained more practically relevant demonstrations of diverse digital practices. It is also noteworthy that discussions about what *tasks* that are relevant in TE received quite a lot of attention. The third seminar focused on the value of taking a research-based approach to developing PDC in TE. Approximately 70 teacher educators from campus and schools as well as student teachers contributed with specific presentations or panel discussions during the seminars. This was done to take advantage of the established and relevant competencies in the institution and facilitate collective student/faculty/school ownership to the project with research as one important mediating resource.

Synthesizing

The three vignettes have demonstrated heterogeneity and potential tensions among the many participants in the LUDO project. Also in the next phases of the project, LUDO will be particularly sensitive to the tensions and sometimes contradictions that come with formative interventions. A key challenge identified through interviews with colleagues is that PDC as concept is vague (see also our discussion on quality and vague concepts in Chapter 3). In the initial phase, LUDO used the PDC framework developed for teachers and teacher educators (see Chapter 6) to promote a shared understanding of the concept. The project group considered it as valuable because it challenges an instrumental understanding of digitalization while at the same time seeking to make certain principles visible for a phenomenon that can otherwise be perceived as chaotic or mistaken for simple tool mastery. Some feared that the framework could become a 'straightjacket' and inhibit creative work with operationalizing PDC and promote the quality of education. Others have expressed that it is too abstract and insufficiently anchored in the subjects to make proper sense. Still, the framework appears to give colleagues a direction as it tries to transform their educational practices and increase their educational quality. It is too early to predict how the framework will be adapted and used over time, but lessons learned from the first phase of the project is that it takes time to develop a deep and epistemologically founded understanding of what PDC is in TE. Institutional legitimacy for transformative digitalization is a longitudinal endeavor. A quick fix simply does not exist.

The two cases in combination illustrate how educational quality can be promoted through transformations initiated over time, involving micro, meso, and macro levels of HE (see also Chapters 3 and 4). The chain of quality must be operationalized from exploratory, local practices to institutional, 'horizontal' legitimacy in order to achieve sustainability. The two cases we have reported here display a series of operationalizing 'building blocks', such as a principled approach to tasks that involve problem situations for students and seed funding for collaborative research and development and seminars that bridge experiential and academic knowledge types. But such building blocks must be put together in certain ways in order not to remain a haphazard collection of 'stunts'. For this, we need people, educators, who can commute between contexts and engage in epistemic work across knowledge domains and types. This is what amounts to boundary work and boundary crossing carried out by collaborating boundary crossers (Engeström, Y., Engeström, R., & Kärkkäinen, 1995), a vital construct in cultural-historical activity theory (CHAT) as well as a prerequisite for developing PDC.

References

Aldersley, S. F. (1995). "Upward Drift" Is Alive and Well: Research/Doctoral Model Still Attractive to Institutions. *Change: The Magazine of Higher Learning, 27*(5), 51–56.

Bassey, M. (2010). A Solution to the Problem of Generalisation in Educational Research: Fuzzy Prediction. *Oxford Review of Education, 27*(1), 5–22. doi:10.1080/03054980123773

Brevik, L. M. (2016). The Gaming Outliers: Does Out-of-School Gaming Improve Boys' Reading Skills in English as a Second Language? In E. Elstad (Ed.), *Educational Technology and Polycontextual Bridging* (pp. 39–62). Rotterdam; Boston; Taipei: SENSE Publishers.

Brevik, L. M., Gudmundsdottir, G., Lund, A., & Strømme, T. A. (2019). Transformative Agency in Teacher Education: Fostering Professional Digital Competence. *Teaching and Teacher Education, 86,* doi: 10.1016/j.tate.2019.07.005.

Csapó, B., & Funke, J. (Eds.). (2017). *The Nature of Problem Solving: Using Research to Inspire 21st Century Learning.* Paris: OECD Publishing.

Daus, S., Aamodt, P. O., & Tømte, C. (2019). *Profesjonsfaglig digital kompetanse i lærerutdanningene. Undersøkelse av tilstand, holdninger og ferdigheter ved fem grunnskolelærerutdanninger.* Oslo: NIFU.

Engeström, Y. (1987). *Learning by Expanding: An Activity – Theoretical Approach to Developmental Research.* Helsinki: Orienta-konsultit.

Engeström, Y. (2011). From Design Experiments to Formative Interventions. *Theory & Psychology, 21*(5), 598–628. doi:10.1177/0959354311419252

Engeström, Y., Engeström, R., & Kärkkäinen, M. (1995). Polycontextuality and Boundary Crossing in Expert Cognition: Learning and Problem Solving in Complex Work Activities. *Learning and Instruction, 5,* 319–336.

Facer, K. (2011). *Learning Futures. Education, Technology and Social Change.* London; New York, NY: Routledge.

Haapasaari, A., Engeström, Y., & Kerosuo, H. (2014). The Emergence of Learners' Transformative Agency in a Change Laboratory Intervention. *Journal of Education and Work.* doi:10.1080/13639080.2014.900168

Haapasaari, A., & Kerosuo, H. (2015). Transformative Agency: The Challenges of Sustainability in a Long Chain of Double Stimulation. *Learning, Culture, and Social Interaction, 4,* 37–47. doi:10.1016/j.lcsi.2014.07.006

Hoholm, T. (2009). *The Contrary Forces of Innovation: An Ethnography of Innovation Processes in the Food Industry.* (PhD) BI Norwegian School of Management.

Jenset, I. S., Klette, K., & Hammerness, K. (2018). Grounding Teacher Education in Practice around the World: An Examination of Teacher Education Coursework in Teacher Education Programs in Finland, Norway, and the United States. *Journal of Teacher Education, 69*(2), 184–197.

Lillejord, S., & Børte, K. (2014). *Partnerships in Teacher Education. An Overview of Research.* Oslo: Kunnskapssenter for utdanning.

Lund, A. (2008). Wikis: A Collective Approach to Language Production. *ReCALL, 20*(1), 35–54.

Lund, A. (2016). I Am Connected, Therefore I Am: Polycontextual Bridging in Education. In E. Elstad (Ed.), *Educational Technology and Polycontextual Bridging* (pp. 129–145). Rotterdam, NL: SENSE Publishers.

Lund, A., & Eriksen, T. M. (2016). Teacher Education as Transformation: Some Lessons Learned from a Center for Excellence in Education. *Acta Didactica Norge, 10*(2), 53–72.

Lund, A., & Hauge, T. E. (2011). Designs for Teaching and Learning in Technology Rich Learning Environments. *Nordic Journal of Digital Literacy, 4,* 258–271.

Munthe, E., & Rogne, M. (2015). Research Based Teacher Education. *Teaching and Teacher Education, 46*, 17–24.

Murray, J., & Male, T. (2005). Becoming a Teacher Educator: Evidence from the Field. *Teaching and Teacher Education, 21*(2), 125–142.

Nielsen, B. S., & Nielsen, K. A. (2016). Critical Utopian Action Research: The Potentials of Action Research in the Democratisation of Society. In H. P. Hansen, B. S. Nielsen, N. Sriskandarajah, & E. Gunnarsson (Eds.), *Commons, Sustainability, Democratization* (pp. 90–120). New York, NY: Routledge.

Ryan, R. M., & Deci, E. L. (2000). Self-determination Theory and the Facilitation of Intrinsic Motivation, Social Development, and Well-Being. *American Psychologist, 55*(1), 68–78.

Säljö, R. (2010). Digital Tools and Challenges to Institutional Traditions of Learning: Technologies, Social Memory and the Performative Nature of Learning. *Journal of Computer Assisted Learning, 26*(1), 53–64.

Sannino, A. (2015). The Emergence of Transformative Agency and Double Stimulation: Activity-based Studies in the Vygotskian Tradition. *Learning, Culture, and Social Interaction, 4*, 1–3. doi:10.1016/j.lcsi.2014.07.001

Somekh, B. (2005). *Action Research: A Methodology for Change and Development: A Methodology for Change and Development.* Maidenhead: McGraw-Hill Education.

Sundquist, P., & Olin-Scheler, C. (2013). Classroom vs. Extramural English: Teachers Dealing with Demotivation. *Language & Linguistics Compass, 7*(6), 329–338. doi:10.1111/lnc3.12031

Vestøl, J. M., & Lund, A. (2017). Co-configuring Design Elements and Quality Aspects in Teacher Education: A Research Agenda. In M. Peters, B. Cowie & I. Menter (Eds.), *A Companion to Research in Teacher Education* (pp. 725–739). Singapore: Springer.

Yin, R. (2009). *Case Study Research, Design and Methods.* Thousand Oaks, CA: Sage Publications.

8 Can we educate students for a future we do not know?

David Olson, in his book on pedagogical reform and schools as basically normative and culturally reproducing institutions, made the keen observation that "No society educates its young to live in a different society" (Olson, 2003, p. 292). A similar reflection was offered by Chris Dede in his remark that "The most dangerous experiment we can conduct with our children is to keep schooling the same at a time when every other aspect of our society is dramatically changing" (Dede, 1997, p. n/a). Keeping with the 'transformative terminology' used in the present volume, both scholars sketch a problem situation (S1) – and a daunting one at that: how do we educate students for a future we do not know? Also, implicit in their observations is the perception of educational institutions as inert (as we briefly discussed in Chapter 1).

Without resorting to crystal balls, what we do know is that our future will be increasingly more digitalized. And with digitalization comes fundamental challenges involving, among many, education as a democratic endeavor, equity and ethics, networked lives and cognitive augmentation, and – very possibly – a fundamental change in what it means to be human (Harari, 2017; Tegmark, 2017). How can HEs cope with this? What resources can HEIs muster, make available, and put to productive epistemic work? Throughout this book, we have sought to raise some fundamental issues we see as pressing in order for HEs to cater to future generations; digitalization and its epistemological implications, digital resources as cultural artifacts, implications of digitalization for educational quality, and the need for professional digital competence (PDC) as an agentive, quality- and context-sensitive as well as transformative capacity. Empirically, we have often used teacher education as an analytical lens to examine challenges and practices in HE, but the references literature covers a plethora of academic and professional disciplines. Throughout the volume, transformation and transformative agency have formed the guiding principles. We have argued that HE urgently needs to cope with, appropriate, and engage in transformative endeavors in times that are changing due to the emergence, impact, and pervasiveness of digitalization.

However, we acknowledge, but resist the temptation to engage in more concrete assumptions, conjecture or 'best guesses' that often turn out to be perceived as normative and/or immediately obsolete. The turnover rate of digital resources and practices is so rapid that the 'old' academic adage of reflection and with reflective practitioners (Schön, 1983) is more topical than ever. Still, some trends and possible futures form on the horizon, and HEs cannot afford to wait them out. Like Keri Facer (2011) says of schools, also HEs must recognize their role "as a prefigurative space for socio-technical futures" (p. 127). As this space is increasingly digitalized, limitations in space, time, and cultural context are suspended and borders between HEs and local and global communities are perforated.

Numerous reports, especially from the policy sector, aim to outline trends where technologies meet innovation and education (see, e.g., Adams Becker et al., 2017; OECD, 2018, for influential and recent examples). These reports are quite unison in what they recognize and emphasize as particularly relevant issues for HEIs – that digitalization is changing innovation, teaching, and research practices. This involves cultural transformation for HEIs, partly by developing student-centered, personalized, and collaborative learning environments, and partly by redesigning and developing learning spaces that go beyond the institution and involve commercial interests. This latter point is one that is, and will continue to be, fiercely debated (Ellis & McNicholl, 2015). Another dimension that will represent fundamental challenges is concerned with ethics when machine learning, robotics, and artificial intelligence (AI) interface with human agents. One of the 'wicked challenges' that permeates these issues is "Rethinking the role of educators" (Adams Becker et al., 2017, p. 3). In the current volume, our response has been the cultivation of transformative agency in both educators and students, especially when they engage in joint educational and epistemic work.

In Table 8.1, we summarize some of the 'digital issues' we have discussed in this volume. In the left-hand column, we list some current features of epistemic work following digitalization. In relation to each issue, we point to potential educational benefits and risks. The societal needs outlined in the right-hand column place the educational benefits and risks in a broader societal context. The table can be seen as a

Table 8.1 Current features of epistemic work following digitalization

Digital issues	Potential benefits	Potential risks	Societal needs
Internet gives access to enormous amounts of information.	Just-in-time information. Align information resources with the context, interest, and competence level of the learner. Juxtaposing different versions and perspectives. Incentive for developing constructing productive search strategies.	Drowning in digital archives. Aimless searching. Hard to distinguish between verifiable and fake information. Encourages plagiarism.	Lifelong, critical learning. Critical literacy. Multi-perspective problem-solving. Knowledge about how to use sources.
People with internet access can easily share experiences, questions, information, knowledge, and perspectives.	Give students access to diverse voices and perspectives. Co-construction of knowledge and critical questioning. More mutuality, reciprocity, and collaboration. More student active learning. Promote in-depth learning. Promote democracy in education.	Political and social surveillance. Corporations gathering information from people's online use. Fake news and "Influencers" detrimental to trust and involvement in online practices.	Linking minds, hands, and hearts for developing global equality and democracy. Collective intelligence and large-scale collaboration to take on global challenges (climate, health, wealth distribution).
People can easily express themselves by combining multiple modalities and interacting with artifacts.	Teachers and students can design and participate in digitally augmented learning environments and learning trajectories. Affords working with complex phenomena and wicked problems. New ways of documenting competencies.	HE lacks criteria and know-how about how to assess new digital expressions of students' competencies. Artifacts with intentions and persuasive power can override human agency.	Engaging in creative processes, innovation, and interaction with humans and artifacts.

(*Continued*)

Table 8.1 (Continued)

Digital issues	Potential benefits	Potential risks	Societal needs
People's access to internet invites HE to develop a variety of flexible educational models and approaches.	Administration can be made more agile and individually relevant. Adaptive, personalized learning environments and assessment. Suspended constraints in space, time, and participation. Easy to produce and share digital learning resources.	Students are left too much to themselves, procrastinate, or drop out. Originally, comprehensive and longitudinal programs become fragmented and superficial modules. Impersonal networks replace learning communities. Suspension of boundaries between work and leisure. When anyone can create digital resources, the quality might be low.	Develop sustainable educational models aligned with needs in working life and local communities.

snapshot of the current state of affairs and can be used as a point of departure for a few more future-oriented issues we briefly discuss on the last pages. It might help leaders and teachers of HE who need to exercise agency over digitalization to decide in which direction educational practices should be transformed. Such decisions are not taken in a vacuum by individual teachers. HE institutions (HEIs) need to consider transformative initiatives in light of the overall responsibility of HE. According to Biesta (2009), HE should both socialize students in knowledge-intensive contexts, qualify them for working life, and be an arena for personal growth. We will add that HE also needs to take more general societal needs into account when transformative initiatives are considered and implemented.

Moving from the current state of affairs to a more future-oriented perspective, the borderline between science and science fiction becomes precarious. Still, research-based forays into territories where not every detail is known are worth-paying attention to. So, what is on the horizon in the not too distant future that HE students, teachers, and leadership must consider, prepare for, and perhaps oppose? No future is given or predetermined but largely shaped by human actors. So, how can we design HE systems and educational programs and activities that are not confined by an 'orthodox' vision of the future: "myopic, largely implausible, and highly selective", according to Facer (2011, p. 87)?

We admit that we are selective when we in the following engage in the hazardous effort of eliciting and condensing insights from scholars (especially Facer, 2011; Harari, 2017; Tegmark, 2017) who either adopt an educational view of the future or envision future challenges that relate to fundamental epistemic and educational (in the broad sense) concerns.

Epistemologies

Let us start by revisiting issues of epistemology (and ontology) as introduced in Chapter 1. We argued that digitalization already impacted on how we come to know through extended, embedded, and embodied relations between humans and digital artifacts. Future-oriented scholarly literature points to significantly increase in computing power, more sophisticated AI, and continued hybridization of humans and artifacts. HE students and educators are increasingly connected and embedded in an assemblage of networks of agents and artifacts. Such networks represent 'collective intelligence' (Lévy, 1997/1999). The traditional relationship between the individual student and the text-book becomes 'outsourced' and 'collectivized'. This and similar trends demonstrate how networks will become the dominant metaphor for personal, social, and institutional capital (Ekbia & Nardi, 2017; Facer, 2011).

But the individual mind is also affected. For example, the pharmaceutical industry and the fields of pharmacogenetics and genetic engineering can turn our minds and bodies into interfaces with knowledge as we are augmented with enhanced memory and better concentration. Cognition-enhancing 'smart drugs' are already produced (Facer, 2011), similar to the more traditional 'doping' found in sports. The result is an augmentation of the self. Where in the past it has proved possible to buy oneself into prestigious HEIs, new capital might come in the form of students' artificially enhanced cognitive power. How will HEIs cope with issues of equity and democratic participation when students appear as more or less valuable 'wetware' (Ekbia & Nardi, 2017) in the epistemic production? Why to upgrade and transform the organization if the upgrading and transformation can be carried by the augmented student? Will we see a future of radical inequality instead of new opportunities for all?

The prosthetic industry furnishes us with body parts superior to the ones we need to replace. And these industries also develop artificial 'skin' that can respond to touch. Thus, haptic technologies emerge where active touch results in kinesthetic or physical feedback combined with computer visualizations. 'Feeling' or 'sensing' our networked experiences will blur the distinctions between physical and virtual representations. The implications for, e.g., surgeons and veterinarians immediately come to mind, but haptic interface might on a more general level suspend boundaries between academic and vocational work, between epistemic and physical work, and between imagining and actually producing prototypes and models.

Partly embodied in, but also separated from human carriers, AI is in rapid development. Hitherto, human strongholds such as natural language (including translation), intuition, and creativity have remained inaccessible to integrate in even the most sophisticated algorithms. With AI programming new devices with increasing 'human' qualities appear. Hence, the boundaries between computing and thinking, and memorization and learning become blurred. The AI community itself is divided when they consider the speed and end point of this development. Still, the prospect of machines "reaching human level and beyond" (Tegmark, 2017, p. 30) only stops short at the notion of consciousness. This most important discussion is outside the scope of this volume (but see, e.g., Harari, 2017; Tegmark, 2017, and an increasing scholarly literature). We terminate it on a, perhaps comforting, note from Harari (2017): "Over the past half-century there has been immense advance in computer intelligence, but there has been exactly zero advance in computer consciousness" (p. 361).

The emerging dialectics between epistemic work and digitalization transforms our conception of "what intelligence and wisdom mean in an age of digital and cognitive augmentation" (Facer, p. 103). This is the epistemic bottom line that all HEIs, academics, staff, and leadership need to acknowledge and act upon. HE is a "knowledge creating collective built on principles of collegiality and trust" (Ellis & McNicholl, 2015, p. 121), and school is "one of the most important institutions we have to help us build a democratic conversation about the future" (Facer, 2011, p. 28). There are considerable consequences for all involved, but let us briefly focus on the HE students and the HE teachers before we conclude on a note of the ethics involved.

The agentive student and the teacher as designer

According to Facer (2011), "To be 'literate' in our digital environment means to be able to model, to experiment, to visualize, to verbalize" and "to engage with the materials by which representations are produced" (p. 71). True, but not quite sufficient. We have also invoked the need to collaborate and communicate with nonhumans (artifacts) based on conceptual and epistemological insights. If not, we – students as well as educators – risk abdicating from our privileged agency as conscious human beings and leave too much epistemic work to the digital algorithms and fail to judge value and quality against context.

As Tegmark (2017) shows, the vast majority of today's occupations are more or less the same as those that have been around for a century or so, and the one job that makes it into the most frequent occupations list is software development (at number 21). However, in a report from the World Economic Forum (Leopold, Ratcheva, & Zahidi, 2018), the authors assess that "increasing demand in the period up to 2022 are Data Analysts and Scientists, Software and Applications Developers, and Ecommerce and Social Media Specialists, roles that are significantly based on and enhanced by the use of technology" (p. viii). Also expected to grow are roles that leverage distinctively 'human' skills, e.g., customer service workers as well as innovation managers. This indicates that digitalization will not totally alter the job market in the coming years.

Focusing more specifically on future higher education, Ehlers and Kellermann (2019) emphasize four scenarios that the student will encounter. They consist of (1) dealing with complex problem-solving and uncertainty, (2) assembling a trajectory among multiple institutions and a networked learning environment, (3) establishing a space where the student can build and refine a personal portfolio and curriculum in collaboration with peers and educators, and (4) preparing for scenarios 1–3 to be persistent in a lifelong learning perspective.

When combined, the trends emphasize the need to cultivate transformative agency in HE. For students this means to collaboratively take on problem situations (S1) and use them to break out of the status quo, expand their practices, and transform the original S1 as well as themselves in this endeavor. This requires, we further argue, PDC where the principles (see Chapter 6) add up to a series of second stimuli (S2) conducive to such transformation.

And where is the HE teacher in this picture? The monologic deliverer of authorized content and/or 'sage-on-the-stage' is a 'threatened species'. We have come to see teachers as designers (Lund & Hauge, 2011) and agents of learning (Saveri & Chwierut, 2011), and catalysts who instigate, enable, support, participate in, and assess object-oriented and mediated learning processes with diverse outcomes. In practical terms, this involves task designs that activate collaboration, inquiry approaches, active use of research, and adding up to problem spaces (S1) where there may be several alternative responses or solutions to ponder and argue. One example of such a task in second language learning could be to take a text in, e.g., Polish and translate it into English by different digital translators. For the student(s), the task would be to evaluate which version is better and for what reasons. Cheating and plagiarism are not relevant, and the task requires intimate linguistic and discursive knowledge. Or what would 21st-century students of medicine or nursing do to help when cholera broke out in the virtual River City community in 1873? This teleporting/virtual reality task is highly context sensitive with regard to available resources (see Dieterle & Clarke (2008) for details) but highly valid for health personnel working in less than high-tech hospitals in affluent countries.

In addition to creating new types of tasks and assignments, designs also comprise educational approaches and activities conducive to constructing responses to such tasks. And it involves making available or developing artifacts (digital, material, conceptual, discursive, symbolic) with which students and educators enter into research-based collaborative partnerships that can improve epistemic work. Finally, and in line with the previous points, assessment criteria and practices must also be redesigned (see also our example in Chapter 7). There is a fundamental and potentially destructive contradiction between traditional assessment models that rest on individual knowledge documentation (results) and, on the other hand, collaborative knowledge advancement (processes) enhanced by digital resources, i.e., performative competence (Säljö, 2010). This issue is not merely a question of what is 'best' but what type of approach that corresponds with the tasks that emerge in a digitalized society. This 'educational chain' (tasks, activities, artifacts, and assessment) requires HE educators to be *designers* – designers of learning environments as well as learning trajectories. To see teachers as designers does not amount to something radically new in the teaching profession. However, how this metaphor is operationalized in the profession is not always clear.

In recent years, scholarly interest in teaching as involving the design of learning resources, environments, and activities has produced a rich and diverse literature. In this literature, digital resources are often at the heart of or even driving the educational designs. But there is considerable diversity in the way design is conceptualized; sometimes linked to an art form and improvisation, sometimes to scientific and even rather prescriptive approaches, often somewhere in between (see, e.g., Agostinho, Bennett, Lockyer & Harper, 2011; Bower, 2017; Conole, 2008; Goodyear, 2015; Laurillard, 2012; Luckin, 2010; Maina, Craft, & Mor, 2015). In line with our view of diverse knowledge types and logics and our emphasis on educational practices, we consider teaching as a *design praxis*, i.e., where theory and practice form a dialectic unit (Roth & Lee, 2007; Lund & Hauge, 2011). This means that teachers' educational designs are very different from plans; designs are research informed but not prescriptive, and they are open to serendipity and inspired input from students or affordances that emerge from digitalization. In Chapter 4, we presented an educational design for health-care students communicating with clients about sensitive or 'taboo' issues. This health-care design captures the intentions we have outlined here.

And this is where the notion of design dovetails with PDC (see Chapter 6). PDC is highly contextual and requires teachers who can assess the affordances of digital resources and connect them to learning objectives to achieve optimal outcomes. Teachers must assist students in understanding why, when, where, and how to make productive use of digital learning resources and decide which are the most appropriate for the assignments they face. Invoking their PDC, HE teachers must instill students with curiosity, creativity, and scientific approaches to unravel ill-defined problems (Goodyear, 2015). But, as we have already discussed, educational designs will have to prepare for epistemic work where humans and nonhumans collaborate. This is not merely a question of having deep knowledge of the artifacts involved but how we as humans enter into new relationships with, dependencies on, and risks of submitting to very powerful manifestations of digitalization. Thus, we need to bring up – rather superficially, but urgent – issues of ethics and empowerment.

Ethical considerations and dilemmas

According to Tegmark (2017), there are more than 100,000 deaths per year in the US due to bad hospital routines and care. From 2000 to 2013, this number might add up to more than one and a quarter million people. In the same time span, robotic surgery was linked to 144 deaths. Without crunching the numbers further, the rationale for, e.g., driverless transportation (35,000 deaths in the US in 2016) and robotic judges with unbiased (sex, ethnicity) approaches and strictly 'professional' decisions (all law literature and case libraries internalized) seems convincing. But with programmed prejudice or AI learning from historically biased data sets, we might see drones used in genocide and (intentionally or not) racial profiling robots. Haptic (touch-based) technologies create experiences of touch, making it possible to literally mapping one's digital self onto the physical body of somebody else. But such technologies also open up opportunities for modeling and bridging knowing *how* (performative) and knowing *that* (reflection). Genetic engineering and pharmaceutically augmented cognition can cause considerable harm if not intimately linked to ethico-moral aspects of agents and actions that also involve machine learning-based decisions. Harari (2017) reaches an ominous conclusion: "We are about to face a flood of extremely useful devices, tools and structures that make no allowance for the free will of individual humans" (p. 355).

In the near future, such digital technologies will probably not dominate the environments of most HE students and educators. But the HE sector would exercise gross negligence if it does not include such perspectives on a general level as well as what these entails in more subject-specific programs, be it nursing, law, or the social sciences. Concerns with plagiarism, offensive language, measurable learning outcomes, and whether digitalization ruins our ability to read are highly relevant, but pale when we recognize and acknowledge the full impact of digitalization on epistemic practices. This is an S1 on steroids: full of conflicting motives, no obvious way ahead, risk of impasse and surrender, and, thus, outsourcing vital decisions to powerful commercial ventures.

Research communities are keenly aware of the ethics involved, but making research agendas transparent enough and discursively accessible for the general public is difficult. However, studies of how research communities struggle with such issues can inform HE educators and leadership as to how ethical issues can be integrated with issues of digitalization. Suffice to exemplify with Nagy, Wylie, Eschrich, and Finn's (2019) in-depth interviews with 12 scientists working in biotechnology, robotics, and AI. Using Mary Shelley's *Frankenstein* (1818/2018) as a powerful metaphor and ethical reference, they report how the scientists grapple with ethical dilemmas. They find themselves in the midst of issues such as science turning against researcher/user, losing something that is inherently human, and transforming humankind towards an existence where 'traditional' values, norms, knowledge, and social life might dissolve without any clear replacements. Such an S1 cannot be 'solved' – at least not with a 'quick fix' – but can be handled and sought transformed by making use of the vast repertoire of second stimuli (S2) found in human activity from philosophy to genetic engineering and how they discursively connect with students and a larger public.

Throughout this volume, digitalization has been in focus. However, when starting to unpack this phenomenon, we immediately discover implications for epistemology, ethics, concepts of quality, and transformation of educational practices. The result is a crowded focus. The reason is that at the heart of digitalization, we (still) find human agency, admittedly increasingly interdependent with and in symbiosis with digital technologies. We argue that this calls for developing PDC in HE and especially transformative agency enacted by humans. Epistemic work, emotional work, creative work, and communicative work (Ekbia & Nardi, 2017) are the kinds of work that can hardly be fully predetermined by algorithms. In an age of coding and procedures, it may be timely to remind ourselves that many of humankind's greatest achievements or scientific discoveries have come about as something unexpected when looking for something else or even pure accidents. Just check the history behind the discovery of penicillin, quinine, X-rays, the pacemaker, corn flakes, and Viagra (to name a few). Our response to machines that immaculately can adhere to sophisticated algorithms and perform complex operations will be that we are superior cognitive organisms; we can outperform you any time because we make mistakes!

There is a lesson in this that basic research and 'pure' science deserve to be cultivated even more than before the age of digitalization. Such processes require time and patience. In Chapter 1, we – perhaps somewhat condescendingly – referred to the 'inertia' in HE. Maybe we should reconsider and acknowledge the value of moving slowly and reflectively when neoliberalism and accelerating digitalization together challenge the traditions of HEIs as democratic spaces for epistemic work and scientific development.

References

Adams Becker, A., Cummins, M., Davis, A., Freeman, A., Hall Giesinger, C., & Ananthanarayanan, V. (2017). *NMC Horizon Report: 2017 Higher Education Edition*. Austin, TX: The New Media Consortium.

Agostinho, S., Bennett, S., Lockyer, L., & Harper, B. (2011). The Future of Learning Design. *Learning, Media and Technology, 36*(2), 97–99. doi:10.108 0/17439884.2011.553619

Bower, M. (2017). *Design of Technology-Enhanced Learning. Integrating Research and Practice*. Bingley: Emerald Publishing Limited.

Conole, G. (2008). The Role of Mediating Artefacts in Learning Design. In L. Lockyer, S. Bennett, S. Agostinho, & B. Harper (Eds.), *Handbook of Research on Learning Design and Learning Objects: Issues, Applications, and Technologies* (Vol. 1, pp. 188–207). Hershey, PA: IGI Global.

Dede, C. (1997). Written Statement to the PCST Panel. *Public Communication of Science and Technology Conference*. Melbourne, AUS.

Dieterle, E., & Clarke, J. (2008). Multi-user Virtual Environments for Teaching and Learning. In M. Pagani (Ed.), *Encyclopedia of Multimedia Technology and Networking, Second Edition* (pp. 1033–1042). Hershey, PA: IGI Global.

Ehlers, U.-D., & Kellermann, S. A. (2019). *Future Skills. The Future of Learning and Higher Education*. DE: nextskills.org, pp. 2–69.

Ekbia, H. R., & Nardi, B. (2017). *Heteromation and Other Stories of Computing and Capitalism*. Cambridge, MA; London: MIT Press.

Ellis, V., & McNicholl, J. (2015). *Transforming Teacher Education: Reconfiguring the Academic Work*. London; New Delhi; New York; Sydney: Bloomsbury Academic.

Facer, K. (2011). *Learning Futures. Education, Technology and Social Change*. London; New York, NY: Routledge.

Goodyear, P. (2015). Teaching as Design. *Herdsa Review of Higher Education, 2*, 27–50.

Harari, Y. N. (2017). *Homo Deus*. London: Vintage.

Leopold, T. A., Ratcheva, V., & Zahidi, S. (2018). *Future of Jobs Report 2018*. Geneva, CH: World Economic Forum.

Lund, A., & Hauge, T. E. (2011). Designs for Teaching and Learning in Technology Rich Learning Environments. *Nordic Journal of Digital Literacy, 4*, 258–271.

Maina, M., Craft, B., & Mor, Y. (Eds.). (2015). *The Art & Science of Learning Design*. Rotterdam, NE: SENSE Publishers.

Nagy, P., Wylie, R., Eschrich, J., & Finn, E. (2019). Facing the Pariah of Science: The Frankenstein Myth as a Social and Ethical Reference for Scientists. *Science and Engineering Ethics*, 1–23. doi:10.1007/s11948-019-00121-3

OECD. (2018). *OECD Science, Technology and Innovation Outlook 2018. Adapting to Technological and Societal Disruption*. Paris: OECD.

Olson, D. R. (2003). *Psychological Theory and Educational Reform: How School Remakes Mind and Society*. Cambridge: Cambridge University Press.

Säljö, R. (2010). Digital Tools and Challenges to Institutional Traditions of Learning: Technologies, Social Memory and the Performative Nature of Learning. *Journal of Computer Assisted Learning, 26*(1), 53–64.

Saveri, A., & Chwierut, M. (2011). *The Future of Learning Agents and Disruptive Innovation*. Palo Alto, CA: Institute for the Future.

Schön, D. (1983). *The Reflective Practitioner: How Professionals Think in Action*. New York, NY: Basic Books.

Shelley, M. W. (1818/2018). *Frankenstein*. London: Penguin Classics.

Tegmark, M. (2017). *Life 3.0. Being Human in the Age of Artificial Intelligence*. London: Penguin Random House UK.

Index

Note: **Bold** page numbers refer to tables.

'academic capitalism' 4
academic knowledge 101, 104
active learning and digitalization 4, 43, 46, 62, 76
affordances 23–25; as analytical concept 23; and artifacts 23; challenging inertia 67; educational models 58–62; and human–computer interface design 23; investigating 55; review and findings 56–58; 21st-century skills 62–66
agency: need for 3–6; notion of 7; *see also* transformative agency
agentive student as designer 113–115
Akcaoglu, M. 76
appropriation: competence and 71–73; mastery and 71–73
'app smashing' 66
Aristotle 10
artifacts 12, 20–22; and affordances 23; alphabet 21; and cultural significance 20, 21; and digital resources 22; as discursive 21; *vs.* tools 21–22; watch as 21
artificial intelligence (AI) 19, 67, 108

Bakhtin, M. M. 72
Baran, E. 59
Biesta, G. 110
Blomgren, C. 65
Brown, M. G. 60
Buitrago Flórez, F. 63

Castells, M. 23
Center for Professional Learning in Teacher Education (ProTed) 86
Chai, C. S. 74
Chaliès, S. 66
Change Laboratory 96
Chen, Y. 61
Cheng, M. 31–33, 39; forms of transformation 32, 34
Clinton, K. A. 20
cluster concept 30; quality as 29–30
cognition: 12, 14, 18, 116; and context 21, 24; distributed 19; extended 13
competence: and appropriation 71–73; and mastery 71–73
computer-supported collaborative learning (CSCL) 18
context, and cognition 24
critical transformation 32, 34
crowdsourcing 24
cultural-historical activity theory (CHAT) 7, 8, 19, 32, 39, 51, 79, 80, 104

Damsa, C. 44, 49
De Bruyckere, P. 59
Dede, C. 62, 107
"Defining Quality" (Harvey and Green) 30
Department of Teacher Education and School Research (DTESR) (University of Oslo) 86–87;

assessment 87; assignment 87; available resources 87; student activities 87
designer: agentive student as 64, 88–92, 113–115; teacher as 25, 66, 78, 81, 86, 113–115
Dew, J. 36, 37
Dewey, J. 7
didactic digital competence 80
DigCompEdu (European Framework for the Digital Competence of Educators) 74–76
digital artifacts 22
digital bullying 64
digital competence: didactic 80; DigCompEdu 75–76; faces of 73–81; generic 80; professional 77–81; professionally oriented 80; SAMR model 76–77; TPACK 74–75; transformative 81
digitalization 1, 47–48; and active learning 4, 43; competence, mastery, and appropriation 71–73; current features of epistemic work following **109–110**; 'digital competence' 73–81; and educational quality 46–48; and epistemology 6, 10–14; implementing in HE 4–5; institutional leadership of 43; and knowledge work 2; and mass collaboration 24; means to enhance 48; overview 71; risks of 44; *see also* digital technology
digital learning resources 65–66
digital resources 1–2; and artifacts 22; development of 1; and educational design 33–34; theorizing 2; as tools 20
digital technology 55; embeddedness 12, 14; embodied 11–12, 14; embodiment of 11–12; and HE 19; *see also* digitalization
Digital Technology and the Contemporary University (Selwyn) 5
distributed cognition 19
distributed leadership 38
Dixon, S. 66
double stimulation: importance of 18; and transformative agency 8–10

educational design 115
educational improvement, and HEI **37**
educational institutions: "loosely coupled system" 43; teaching and learning practices in 43; *see also* higher education institution (HEI)
educational leadership 39
educational models, and affordances 58–62
educational quality 4, 12, 47–48; and digitalization 46–48; means to enhance 48
educational value 43
education commodification 4
Ehlers, U. -D. 113
Elken, M. 37
Ellis, V. 4
embeddedness, digital technology 12, 14
embodiment of digital technology 11–12
Emirbayer, M. 7
emotional transformation 32, 34
epistemic practices 24, 34, 37, 116
epistemic work 11, 14, 48, 50, 67, 104, 108, **109–110**, 112, 113, 115, 117
epistemology 111–112; defined 10; and digitalization 6, 10–14; embedded digital technology 12, 14; embodied digital technology 11–12, 14; and knowledge 10–11
ethics 107–108, 115–117
European Commission 4, 50; science and knowledge service 62; Skills Agenda for Europe 62
extended cognition 13

Facer, K. 108, 113
flipped classroom 60
Fossland, T. 39, 50
'*Frankenscience*' 67
Frankenstein (Shelley) 116
Future of Jobs Survey 62

Garcia-Huidobro, J. C. 7
generic digital competence 80
Gibson, J. J. 23, 55
Green, B. 73
Green, D. 30

Hamilton, E. R. 76
haptic (touch-based) technologies 116
Harari, Y. N. 19, 24, 112, 116
Harvey, L. 30
Helsinki Developmental Work
    Research (DVR) 96
Heraclitus 9
Hew, K. F. 63
higher education (HE) 58; chain
    of quality in 39; cyberbullying
    in 64; and digital technology 19;
    implementing digitalization in
    4–5; institutional leadership in
    38; institutional legitimization
    in 59; and management 49, 51;
    mobile technology in 60; models
    showing different approaches to
    digitalization in **58**; quality in 28;
    transformative agency in 7–10,
    113–114
higher education institution (HEI):
    educational improvement **37**;
    improvement in overall quality
    of 36; as mass education
    institutions 3; and Norwegian HE
    digitalization 48; plan–do–study–
    act (PDSA) model **37**; quality of
    36; *see also* educational institutions
Hoholm, T. 97, 101
hybridity (digitalization) 11–12

"ICT and Learning: What Does
    Research Say?" module 93
Ilomäki, L. 73
inertia, affordances challenging 67
infinite regress 39–40
information and communication
    technology (ICT) literacy 5, 73
InnoCentive 24
institutional leadership 43
instrumental know-how (*techne*) 10
intellectual transformation 32, 34
Internet-based learning (IBL)
    platforms 63

Jónasson, J. T. 5–6, 12
Journal of Educational Change (JEC) 7

Kantosalo, A. 73
Kellermann, S. A. 113
Kirschner, P. A. 59

knowledge: academic 101, 104; CHAT
    79–80; content 74; and epistemology
    10–11; pedagogical content 74;
    research-based 11, 55, 88, 98;
    technological 74; user-defined 59;
    work and digitalization 2
Koh, J. H. L. 74
Kvernbekk, T. 29, 30

Laaser, W. 66
Lakkala, M. 73
Lankshear, C. 11, 73
Lantz-Andersson, A. 64
Latour, B. 20
leadership: distributed 38;
    educational 39; institutional 38;
    transformative 38
learning: active 4, 43; machine 13,
    108; m-learning (mobile) 58–60, 67
Learning Tools Interoperability (LTI)
    standard 88
Lil Miquela (fictional character) 22
LUDO project 95–104; employing
    teachers from schools in teacher
    education 99–100; from micro
    initiatives to institutional change
    100–103; seed projects 98–99

Macaulay, P. J. R. 64
machine learning 13, 108
McNicholl, J. 4
Major, L. 63
Mäkitalo, Å 7
Makri, A. 65
Male, T. 85
management, and higher education
    49, 51
man–machine hybridity 67
mass collaboration: as affordance 24;
    and digitalization 24
massive open online courses
    (MOOCs) 3–4, 60–61, 67
Mische, A. 7
m-learning 58–60, 67
Murray, J. 85

The Networked Society (Castells)
    23–24
Nordic Institute for Studies in
    Innovation, Research and
    Education (NIFU) 101

Norwegian Centre for ICT in Education 77
Norwegian HE digitalization: and educational quality 44, 46–48; and HEIs 48; macro level 39, 42; meso level 39, 42; teachers' decision of using digital tools 51; White Paper 16 (2016–2017) on Quality Culture in Higher Education 44–49; *see also* digitalization
Norwegian Ministry of Education and Research 44

Objects with Intent (OwIs) 11, 22
Olson, D. 107
open educational resources (OERs) 65
Organization for Economic Cooperation and Development (OECD) 84
Oria 35, 56

Paavola, S. 73
pedagogical courses 52
Pedro, L. 59
performative competence 13
personal transformation 32, 34
physical transformation 32, 34
practical insight (*phronesis*) 10
Pritchard, D. 14
professional digital competence (PDC) 32, 46, 72, 77–81; bridging in-school and out-of-school contexts 91–93; committing to research-based approaches 93–94; developing PDC in teacher education 88–94; DTESR 86–87; integrating different knowledge types 89–91; synthesizing 94–95; and transformative agency in small private online community 86–95
professionally oriented digital competence 80
Puentedura, R. 76

quality: categories of 30; as cluster concept 29–30; in HE 28; management of 38; measurement 29; scholarly literature on 29; as transformation 30–33
Quality 4.0 35
quality culture 38
Quality in Nordic Teaching (QUINT) 86
quality work 38

racial profiling robots 116
Ramberg, K. R. 39, 50
research: -based approaches 93–94; secondary 56
research-based knowledge 55, 88, 98; defined 11; and digitalization 11; *see also* knowledge
robotics 1, 67, 108, 116
Rosenberg, J. M. 76
Royle, K. 59
Rückriem, G. 25

SAMR model *see* Substitution, Augmentation, Modification, and Redefinition (SAMR) model
Sannino, A. 7–8
scaffolding 61
scientific knowledge (*episteme*) 10
"secondary research" 56
Selwyn, N. 5
Shaffer, D. W. 20
Shelley, M. 116
Shulman, L. S. 74
small private online course (SPOC) 88
Snyder, I. 73
STEM subjects 60
Stensaker, B. 37
Sterling, S. 55
Substitution, Augmentation, Modification, and Redefinition (SAMR) model 74, 76–77, 81

TakingITGlobal 24
teacher: augmentation 76; as designer 113–115; modification 76; redefinition 76; substitution 76
teacher education: developing PDC in 88–94; DTESR 86–87; employing teachers from schools in 99–100; LUDO project 95–104;

overview 84–85; PDC and transformative agency in small private online community 86–95; synthesizing 94–95
teaching and learning centers (TLCs) 51–52
'technoliteracy' 73
technological knowledge 74
Technological Pedagogical Content Knowledge (TPACK) framework 73–75
Tegmark, M. 19, 113, 115
thematic identification 45
Toloza, E. 66
tools 20–22; advantages of 20; *vs.* artifacts 21–22; digital resources as 20
transformation: forms of 32; personal 32, 34; physical 32, 34; quality as 30–33
transformative agency 2; and double stimulation 8–10; in HE 7–10; PDC and 86–95; *see also* agency
transformative digital competence 81
transformative leadership 38

Tsai, C. -C. 74
21st-century skills 62–66

University of South-Eastern Norway 96
user-defined knowledge 59

Vestøl, J. M. 30
Virkkunen, J. 7
Vlachopoulos, D. 65
Vygotskian tradition 19
Vygotsky, L. S. 8–10

Washington, E. T. 64
Weick, C. 43
White Paper 16 (2016–2017) on Quality Culture in Higher Education 44–49; teaching and learning centers 51–52
Wikipedia 24
Wittek, L. 29–30
"workforce-development professionals" 35
World Economic Forum 62, 113